Introducing Film

Introducing Film

Graham Roberts
Lecturer in Communications Arts, University of Leeds

and

Heather Wallis
Lecturer in Film Studies, Leeds College of Art and Design

A member of the Hodder Headline Group
LONDON
Co-published in the United States of America by
Oxford University Press Inc., New York

First published in Great Britain in 2001 by
Arnold, a member of the Hodder Headline Group,
338 Euston Road, London NW1 3BH

http://www.arnoldpublishers.com

Co-published in the United States of America by
Oxford University Press Inc.,
198 Madison Avenue, New York, NY10016

Whilst the advice and information in this book are believed to be true and
accurate at the date of going to press, neither the authors nor the publisher
can accept any legal responsibility or liability for any errors or omissions
that may be made.

British Library Cataloguing in Publication Data
A catalogue record for this book is available from the British Library

Library of Congress Cataloging-in-Publication Data
A catalog record for this book is available from the Library of Congress

ISBN 0 340 80742 3 (hb)
ISBN 0 340 76228 4 (pb)

Production Editor: Rada Radojicic
Production Controller: Bryan Eccleshall
Cover Design: Terry Griffiths

Typeset in 11 on 13 pt Palatino by Cambrian Typesetters, Frimley, Surrey
Printed and bound in Malta by Gutenberg Press

What do you think about this book? Or any other Arnold title?
Please send your comments to feedback.arnold@hodder.co.uk

This book is dedicated to
Shirley Roberts
and the memory of Fred and Freda Wallis

They first showed us 'the kingdom of the shadows'

Contents

Acknowledgements

The authors would like to thank:

Lesley Riddle at Arnold;
Prof. Philip Taylor, Robin Brown, David Gauntlett, Stephen Hay
and Isobel Rich at the ICS, University of Leeds;
Graeme Brown at LCAD;
students at both the University of Leeds and LCAD who have
been more or less willing but never less than stimulating guinea
pigs for all of the material contained herein;
Mr and Mrs Smith, Ellen, Ros and Steve Day; Eleanor 'Cakey'
Beaumont, Annie, Harvey Rachel and Simon Black, Bill Wallis,
Brian Wallis and Patsy Roberts; and Charlotte and Sam.

This book would not have been written without the various inspi-
rations, interruptions and emotional support supplied by all of
the above.

Introduction
Why study film?

> I have been in the kingdom of the shadows . . . If only you
> knew how strange it is to be there.
>
> (Maxim Gorky, 1896)

Gorky's response to film was one of the first ever published. The mixture of awe, fascination, curiosity and intrigue as to what film is and what it means has been implanted in the minds of most spectators of this most emotionally powerful of mediums. This book is designed to introduce students from any disciplinary background to the basic body of knowledge and many of the conceptual frameworks that enable us to study film. We also aim to enable any viewer to gain some insight into the making and consuming of films which will aid their appreciation of 'the movies'. We hope, as the current A-Level syllabus puts it, to 'deepen . . . understanding, appreciation and enjoyment of film'. Our manifesto begs the question: 'why study film?'

1. Cinema is an essential part of popular culture. It also makes a crucial contribution to the content and grammar of popular culture. Cinema has produced the canonical texts upon which so much of today's visual culture is built and to which so much of contemporary culture is indebted.

We believe that not only was film the major art form of the twentieth century, but also that it remains the cultural form of greatest significance at the beginning of the new millennium. Consumption of film remains the single most popular and important entertainment experience whether it be through (globally reviving) cinemas, video, films screened on television or subscription via television and multimedia. The 'art form' which might conceivably challenge film in the twenty-first century – i.e. computer games – is completely reliant on the forms and language of cinema to engage its audience. The oft-predicted great art form of the future is in essence a more interactive version of 'movies'.

2. *Cinema is a national, multinational and global institution.* It is essential for an active citizen to gain knowledge and understanding of how cinema functions as a business and under which institutional constraints. Viewers will gain an understanding of particular films if they can locate them within the specific institutions which produced them and by placing those institutions within their economic social and cultural contexts.

3. *Film was, is and will remain a medium of messages and values.* The viewer can develop a mature and subtle understanding of this process of making meaning through application of critical approaches (and evaluating those approaches). It is also essential to develop a critical understanding of our own participation as consumers of so powerful a medium and to acquire an ability to identify messages and values, especially in the area of representation.

4. *Film is a language.* 'A language far more complex than words', as the great cinematographer Conrad Hall put it. All films can be better understood with a grasp of common threads of expression and tradition. All viewers can gain from knowledge and understanding of how films work formally and stylistically through critical understanding of the options available to film-makers. This understanding will lead to increased engagement. In addition, the study of film will develop skills to identify and explore your own response and to communicate those responses.

5. *Textual and contextual analysis is a transferable skill.* Critical approaches to vast amounts of information is a required skill in the new (or any) millennium. Studying film is as good a way as any of acquiring such skills and far more entertaining than most.

Finally, we should not forget that film is an entertainment medium. Whenever a film-maker, theorist, or political regime forgets this they lose their audience. Without the audience films are merely lights flickering in the dark for no purpose. That being said there is no reason to doubt that a well-informed critical audience can be a factor in an artistically thriving and stimulating cinema.

Graham Roberts and Heather Wallis
January 2001

1 Mise en scène

The proper use of light can embellish and dramatise every object.

(Josef von Sternberg)

The language of film is constructed from three elements:

- what is to be filmed – traditionally called *mise en scène;*
- how it is filmed – cinematography;
- how that material is put together (usually to tell coherent stories) – editing.

Cinematography (literally: writing in movement) is basically a form of *photography* (writing in light). Much as photography must have an object, cinema must begin with something to film. The film-maker(s) must place something before the camera. This may be done by the act of arranging objects within the viewing range of the photographic device and/or placing the camera before objects either found 'on location' or arranged for filming. Therefore, let us begin – as we must – with what is placed in front of the camera: *mise en scène*. The French term *mise en scène* means literally 'placed on stage.' It was borrowed from theatre by French critics and became a well-known term due to extensive use by the *Cahiers du Cinéma* writers in the 1950s (see Chapters 6 and 9 for a discussion of the significance of their theories). *Mise en scène* is what cinema has in common with theatre. However, cinema goes beyond placing things – it films them too.

This chapter aims to introduce the reader to the elements of *mise en scène* and will illustrate how the different elements of setting, costume and make-up, figure, expression, movement and lighting aid the construction of meaning. To illustrate the power of *mise en scène* we have included detailed guided readings of the opening sections of *Metropolis* (Lang, Germany, 1926) and *Raiders of the Lost Ark* (Spielberg, USA, 1981). This chapter will also introduce one of the key areas of intellectual debate about film: realism versus formalism. The chapter concludes with a series of questions designed to help structure *mise en scène* analysis.

All film-making is a matter of choices. Everything that we see on screen has been *placed* – note *placed* – before the camera. The question becomes 'why?' and 'to what effect?'

The elements of *mise en scène* are as follows:

* setting
* costume and make-up
* figure, expression and movement
* lighting.

SETTING

Setting gives us a sense of place and time. It can be used to create a sense of historical reality, e.g. the computer-enhanced Roman Coliseum in *Gladiator* (Scott, USA, 2000); or it can symbolise a character's state of mind, e.g. *The Cabinet of Dr Caligari* (Weine, Germany, 1919). Here the set is constructed from painted buildings and streets with weirdly distorted angles and shapes. The distortions in the set design symbolise the mental disturbance and social chaos of the characters. Alternatively (and perhaps most frequently) the setting can appear to be natural, the everyday background of house, office, city, street where the characters live, or it can create the sense of the fantastic and other-worldly often seen in science fiction films like *Star Wars* (Lucas, USA, 1977) or *Alien* (Scott, UK, 1979). Whatever kind of setting is used in a film, even if it appears to be an everyday, ordinary apartment where the characters live, is important and worthy of analysis. It can provide us with information, not just about where the action takes place and when, but about mood, characters, type of story and the genre of the film. Shots of Monument Valley, dusty and magnificent, a saloon bar or a homestead isolated on the prairie immediately signal to the viewer that the film is a Western. Thus from the setting a whole sequence of meanings and expectations are created.

In *Intolerance* (USA, 1916) D. W. Griffith, along with his cameramen Billy Bitzer and Karl Brown and his team of hand-picked designers, conspired to create the most expensive film ever made. The intertwined stories of man's inhumanity to man cover the whole of human history. The most spectacular scenes come within the Babylon episode, for which the entire city was constructed in one huge set. Here the audience was transported to another time and place. This world is pure fantasy but it is presented with painstaking (not to say very costly) realism.

In *One from the Heart* (USA, 1982) Francis Coppola, with cine-matographer Vittorio Storora, produced perhaps the most expensive mistake in cinema history. The whole affair cost so much that Coppola had to liquidate his production company to pay off the debts incurred in building the sets. The fact that the whole film was shot on sets and that these sets – from the title sequence onwards – clearly are sets, is a deliberate attempt to place the viewer outside of the action. We know (and the film-makers want us to know) that it is all fabricated.

Here, right at the beginning of our study of film, we are confronted with a basic schism within film-making and indeed theorising about film: formalism and/or expressionism versus realism.

Formalism stresses the importance of form over content in film-making. It prioritises how things are shown rather than simply what takes place. Formalists consider that film is art when it goes beyond a representation of reality to become something more than reality. It is an act of personal expression, just like a painting. The fact that it is unrealistic helps rather than hinders its status as a work of art by making the viewer conscious of the way it has been constructed.

Expressionism, or German Expressionism, is a term borrowed from the Expressionist movement in art in the early part of the twentieth century, which rejected realist modes of representation. Expressionist films are highly stylised. Hallmarks of this style include oblique camera angles, distorted bodies and shapes, bizarre settings and stylised lighting design, with extreme contrast between light and dark creating dramatic shadows (known as chiaroscuro – see Lighting section below). Expressionist films were equally surreal in their subject matter, projecting on screen a char-acter's subjective and often mad world.

Realism, on the contrary, claims that film's strength is its special relationship with the real world. Of all the art forms film has the ability to look most like real life. If we look at a painting we can see the canvas, the brushstrokes, the texture of the paint. In other words what we see is obviously constructed by man. Similarly, with theatre the 'falsity' of a performance is ever present – in the curtain, the visible lights, the scene changes, and the actors appearing at the end – no longer in character – to take their bows. These aspects of the theatrical experience make it very clear that what we are seeing is not real but a representation of life. Still, we do not spend the entire performance after Macbeth has murdered Duncan muttering that he is not really dead. We willingly suspend our disbelief for the duration of the performance and enter into the world of make-believe. This process is made very easy for us with film. The artificial elements of construction can all but disappear leaving us with something that looks so natural and life-like that we can forget that what we are viewing is a representation (written, performed, filmed and edited) of reality, not real. As cinema developed (especially in Hollywood) realism became the dominant style (see Continuity Editing, Chapter 3, pp. 40ff.). It prioritises content and subject matter over form; therefore it could be called the style of no style.

Of the examples of setting above *The Cabinet of Dr Caligari* belongs to the German Expressionist tradition, D. W. Griffith's 'Babylon' in *Intolerance* is in the realist tradition, and Francis Coppola's *One from the Heart* is in the formalist tradition. Choices in the *mise en scène* therefore are instrumental in creating the overall style of the film.

COSTUME AND MAKE-UP

Costumes are in a sense part of the set. The clothes worn on set indicate period and social milieu. Costume is also an instant indicator of social class, cultural background and of character traits. Whether we like it or not people make instant judgements by observing dress. This may well be because we have so little time to explore other means of forming opinions. The process of watching a movie – at least for the first time – requires the viewer to make instant judgements. The film-makers (including the actors) can push the viewer into certain verdicts by the choices of how they dress and set their characters. Members of the audience may of course choose to ignore and subvert the 'preferred meaning' offered. This process is discussed in Chapter 10.

Costume, which includes make-up and personal props, gives the viewer a sense of place, time and characterisation as well as type of story and genre. Changes in costume can highlight changes in a characters feelings and/or situation. For example in *Titanic* (Cameron, USA, 1998) the character of Rose (Kate Winslet) is first presented to us by a very deliberate focus on costume. We see a detail shot (taken from above) of her gloved hand emerging from a car. The camera maintains its aerial position as she steps out of the car so that she is almost totally obscured by the brim of her elaborate hat. Her costume is being signalled as the most important aspect of her character at this point in the film – it separates her from the mass of 'poor' characters and defines her class and status. In a later scene when Jack (Leonardo Di Caprio) paints her she lets down her hair and takes her costume off. Thus the viewer can infer she is casting off the codes and conventions of her class which are symbolised in her dress. After the sinking of the ship we see her bedraggled and unkempt in steerage with the other third-class passengers who have survived. Her costume is still being used to represent status and social position but these things have changed as she has rejected the world of wealth and privilege. Similarly, in *The Godfather* trilogy (Coppola, USA, 1972, 1974 and 1990) costume is an important indicator of genre but it also helps us to chart the changing fortunes of the characters. Michael Corleone's rise to power in *The Godfather* is reflected in his ever more expensive-looking clothes as Vito Corleone's parallel relinquishment of power is revealed in his increasingly relaxed ones. Costume can therefore indicate a character's (changing) status in the world, their feelings about themselves, the feelings they wish to inspire in others. Costume can also be a trademark (for super heroes and comedians), e.g. various incarnations of Superman and Batman or Charlie Chaplin's tramp character in *The Gold Rush* (USA, 1925).

Costume includes make-up, which in itself can have many different functions and effects, from creating the glamour of a star to the generic horror of a ghoul. Make-up is important in maintaining the illusion created by a particular setting: for example, the glisten of sweat on the gladiators in *Gladiator*; the dusty faces of cowboys and the war paint of Indians in many Westerns; the blue-white faces of the characters freezing to death in *Titanic*. Make-up is also important in creating the illusion that time has passed, e.g. Kane's ageing process in *Citizen Kane* (Welles, USA, 1940) or the final scene in *The Godfather Part 3* where costume and make-up together create the effect of many years having passed.

FIGURE, EXPRESSION AND MOVEMENT

The word 'figure' covers a range of possibilities. It is most likely to be a character but it could also be an animal or an object. Movement looks at the position and movement of characters or objects within the frame. We generally think of figure, expression and movement as 'acting', which is made up of the visual elements of body language, appearance and facial expressions (as well as the sound elements of voice and sound effects) but it can incorporate other things.

The way figures stand or move is a key element in the formation of 'character'. In our day-to-day dealing with others we judge by observing body language. Cinema is moving pictures (cinematography – writing in movement), so the way a character moves is of central importance, particularly if they are a cultural icon (see Chapters 7 and 8).

There are various ways in which a film-maker can use position and movement within the frame to create meaning.

- If, for instance, a character or object is placed within the foreground of a shot, the viewer is likely to attach more importance to it than to something in the background of a shot.
- A moving body or object against a stationary background will automatically draw our attention (as it does in real life).
- Characters or objects positioned evenly within the frame will create a balanced feel to the shot. If all the figures are at one end this will create an imbalance for the eye and an unsettling effect.
- Positioning of characters within the frame can indicate the relationship between them. Characters engaged in an argument might for example be positioned at either edge of the frame, the space between them indicating their emotional distance from each other.

In a scene from *The Comedy Strip Presents: 'Strike'* (Richardson, UK, 1984) – a British television parody of how Hollywood distorts history, not to mention the intentions of writers and directors – Peter Richardson, playing 'Al Pacino', is faced with pages and pages of text to learn. He rejects the task, claiming: 'I can say all that by the way I stand.'

At the end of *The Searchers* (Ford, USA, 1956) the inability of the hero, Ethan (John Wayne) to belong to the civilised family group that he has struggled to restore is expressed in a single shot. We see him doubly framed, at the centre of the screen and through the door of the homestead, as he turns and walks away from the newly restored order that closes the film. In this single shot, position and movement within the frame express all the ambiguities and conflicts in Ethan's character and the film as a whole. The shot both provides a sense of closure (family order is restored) and simultaneously undermines this closure because the central character is excluded and left to an uncertain future.

Facial expression is an important part of acting, far more important to cinema than to theatre. The audience can and does get much closer to its object of scrutiny. It was argued that expression was more important in cinema than television, not least because the expressions projected were so much bigger. This is less tenable an argument now that so much 'cinema' is consumed via a TV screen and that so much television is built on the grammar of the tight close up (often as a 'talking head'). What is certain is that much screen time is spent focusing on the faces of actors. The audience observes these faces closely because of a natural tendency to identify and be interested in the faces of other people. Whether it is true or not we tend to believe that 'eyes are the mirrors of the soul'. We also tend to follow eye movements; thus a film-maker can draw attention to something or change a 'point of view' by moving the camera to match these changes (see Chapters 3 and 5).

LIGHTING

Photography is writing in light. It is worth remembering that no object can be seen, never mind filmed, without light. Film cannot be viewed without some form of light source. Thus light is crucial: no light no picture. Film lighting does more however than simply enable us to see the action. In conjunction with the other elements of film language it aids the viewer to construct meaning from the images. The film-maker's use of lighting will, for example suggest who/what is the key figure in a scene as well as how we should read the mood of a scene. It can be an indication of the genre of the film and is often central in the creation of mystery, tension and suspense.

Lighter and darker areas within the frame help create meaning by guiding the viewer's eyes to certain objects and actions. Bright illumination literally highlights an area of the screen thus drawing attention to key elements. Conversely the use of shadows can produce a sense of suspense about what might be revealed later.

The way in which an image is lit is central therefore to its impact.

There are four major features of film lighting:

- intensity
- source
- direction
- colour.

Intensity

Hard lighting creates clearly defined shadows, harsh textures and crisp edges. Soft lighting blurs contours, softens textures and creates gentler contrasts which are often seen as 'natural'.

Source

The light source can be natural (sunlight, firelight) or artificial (lamps). The source of light is usually motivated – in other words we can see where it is supposed to be coming from (sunlight streaming through a window or lamps on the bedside table). Often the effect of 'natural' light was created with lamps in order to provide enough light with which to film, although as cinema progressed faster film stocks (that need less light) were developed, which allowed cinematographers greater freedom of choice. A consequence of this was that film-makers were less restricted to studio-based film-making (where sets could be designed to accommodate the huge and heavy arc lights required) and had the option of filming on location. The directors of the French New Wave, for example, filmed on the streets and in their own apartments. They were enabled to do this because of the lighter cameras developed in the USA for documentary shooting that did not require elaborate lighting rigs. This meant that the budget for the films could be much lower (no set design, smaller crew, less equipment), enabling first-time directors to have a go. These practical and technical factors had at least as much impact on the style of the 'New Wave' as the many theories of its directors (see Chapter 6).

Direction

This refers to the path of light to the object lit.

- Front lighting will flatten an image and remove shadows.
- Side lighting highlights features, e.g. nose or cheekbones, by casting shadows.
- Back lighting defines depth by distinguishing an object from its background.
- Under lighting distorts features.
- Top lighting 'bathes' an object (often a star) to create an aura of glamour.

Hollywood in its classical period (see Chapter 5) developed a system of using three light sources in each shot known as the Three Point Lighting system:

- the key light – usually the brightest and shining diagonally from the front;
- the back light – helping to counteract the 'unnatural' look of the key, coming from the rear (and usually above);
- the fill light – helping to soften the shadows produced by the key, coming from a position near to the camera.

'High-key' lighting, which uses lots of filler lights to obliterate shadows, has become the norm in most cinema throughout the world. 'Low-key' lighting is created by using only the key and back lights. This technique will produce a sharp contrast of light and dark areas on screen. Very deep distinct shadows are formed. The effect is known – in a term borrowed from painting – as chiaroscuro. *Chiàro* is the Italian word for 'light' and *oscúro* means 'dark'. Extreme use of this technique is most strikingly used in film noir. Film noir (black film) began as a term used by French critics to describe American detective films made in the 1940s and 1950s. These films were not only dark in their subject matter (crime, deceit and human weakness) but also in their look. The style reached its epitome with films such as *The Big Combo* (Joseph Lewis, USA, 1955) and *Touch of Evil* (Welles, USA, 1958). The lighting plans owed much to the deep shadows and harsh contrasts of German Expressionism of the 1920s. It is interesting to note that one of the reasons for the stark, contrasted lighting schemes in these movies was economic. Less complicated lighting plans are cheaper to film.

Colour

We tend not to be aware of the colour of light in film unless we look for it. Naturalism is often created by the use of apparently 'white' light – but much lighting in film is produced by the combination of lights filtered to produce particular colours. Colours carry their own symbolic meanings. We are likely, for example, to associate reds, yellows and orange with warmth, and blues and greys with cold. In *The Piano* (Campion, New Zealand, 1992) the colour of light is instrumental in creating the mood and indicating the state of mind of Ada, the heroine. Scenes of intimacy, happiness and relaxation are delineated by warm amber colours, which provide a stark contrast to the cold blue white light of much of the rest of the film, where we see her struggling with adversity. Similarly, in *Jane Eyre* (Zefferelli, UK, 1996) most of the scenes of Jane's childhood, where we see her in a series of hostile environments, are filmed in cold blue/white light indicating the lack of emotional warmth she experiences. When she arrives at Thornfield Hall she is greeted with warmth and kindness by Mrs Fairfax and this is highlighted by the warm rosy colour of the light, apparently cast by the fire, bathing her face. Analysis of colour symbolism clearly should not be restricted to the area of lighting since it can be extended to the use of colour in the other aspects of *mise en scène*, and also to the choice of black and white or colour film stock (see Chapter 2).

In *Days of Heaven* (Malik, USA, 1978) cinematographer Nestor Almendros created a dream-like state by filming exclusively during the 'magic hour'. This period, when the sun has dropped below the horizon but still illuminates the sky, actually lasts less than 30 minutes each day. The exterior scenes – especially in the fields – are infused with a milky luminescence that suits the rural tale perfectly. Almendros left the film to begin work with Francois Truffaut. Haskell Wexler, a great American cinematographer, eschewed egotism for artistic integrity and finished the film in Almendros' style.

Lighting can also take a leading role as part of the action, as can be seen in *Blade Runner* (Ridley Scott, USA, 1982). The film follows a detective of the future as he tries – reluctantly – to track down a group of 'replicants' (androids on the run) through a futuristic dystopia. In the climactic scene the tables are turned and the hero Deckard (played by Harrison Ford) is being pursued by the final 'replicant'. Shafts of white light penetrate the gloom as Dekard is chased. The cinematographer – Jordan Cronenweth – uses the shafts of light to intensify the impression of threat towards the increasingly desperate hero.

Phillipe Rousselot's cinematography for interior scenes in *Diva* (Beineix, France, 1981) uses a very similar lighting plan – of shafts of light against an intensely dark background. Here, due to a slower pace and the fact that the characters move comfortably, the effect is one of stylised 'cool'.

To conclude, *mise en scène* is the term we use to describe everything we see within a single shot. In terms of film production and film analysis it is distinct and separate from cinematography (film stock, position and movement of the camera) and editing (the joining of shots), although meaning is created from the way these things work in conjunction with each other and with sound. The prominence of (and meanings attached to) costume in the example from *Titanic* were created through the *mise en scène* but also the type of shot that effectively highlights those aspects of the *mise en scène* the film-maker wants us to focus on. The distinctions between the different elements of film language are therefore rather artificial, but having different categories for analysis does help us to approach a film or sequence of film. Breaking it down into its different elements can help us to see how an overall effect is created. When approaching a film or sequence for the purposes of analysis it is very difficult to be simultaneously aware of the editing, the cinematography, the sound and all the different elements of *mise en scène*. It is much easier to approach an extract by looking at a single element, for example lighting, and then to view it again by looking at something else. In this way it is possible to see how meanings are created from the different elements of film language and, how they work in conjunction with each other. To aid this process we have included some questions on *mise en scène* that should act as a guide to analysis at the end of this chapter. The rest of this chapter consists of two readings from two different film sequences that focus on the *mise en scène*.

METROPOLIS (LANG, GERMANY, 1926)

This Expressionist classic opens with images of pistons pumping and wheels spinning, cut with the image of a ticking clock. We are viewing the internal workings of some huge machine. This is the first of many suggestions that the society of Metropolis is mechanised, ordered and controlled. The subsequent images reinforce this idea. 'The Day Shift' is announced in white text against a black background and we then see two sets of workers waiting in ordered ranks before the huge, barred gate of a lift. The setting with its bars has a prison-like quality and this is enhanced by the uniform costume of the workers (black caps, black shirts, black trousers) and their position and movement. All have bowed heads and expressionless faces and when the gates open they move in a choreographed and synchronised manner. They are organised like soldiers but more shuffling and slower, their bowed heads suggesting defeat. The rhythmic quality of their slow march echoes the movement of the pistons in the opening shots indicating that they are part of the same mechanism.

These opening images combine to create the impression of slavery and imprisonment. The workers and their environment seem inhuman, totally devoid of individuality, freedom of choice or movement. The lighting at this point is high-key, allowing us to see the details of the set. Once the bars of the lift have closed the workers are taken down (symbolically) to 'The worker's city, far below the surface of the earth'. Here the setting, with its rectangular shapes, soaring pillars and sharp lines, presents us with the same inhuman quality. It looks both alien and magnificent, the effect enhanced by shafts of light and shadow criss-crossing the enormous structures, the height of which completely dwarfs the workers.

The next title introduces us to a contrasting setting: 'And high above a pleasure garden for the sons of the masters of Metropolis'. For the first time we see movement that looks spontaneous rather than rhythmic as a scantily clad girl runs across the set pursued by Frieder, the hero of the film. The contrast to the inhuman quality of the workers' city is further enhanced by the first 'natural' images. We see a peacock and other exotic birds, plants and the flowing water of the fountain at the centre of the garden. The overwhelming impression created by the jewelled costume and naked flesh of the woman, the mermaid at the centre of the fountain, the

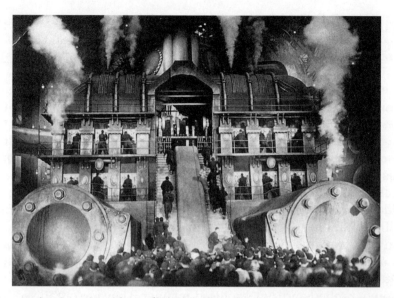

Mise en scène in action, *Metropolis* (1926). Reproduced with permission from BFI Stills, Posters and Designs

game of chase followed by an embrace, is one of decadent pleasure. The garden in fact seems as clearly constructed for a purpose as the worker's city. The juxtaposition of these two contrasting settings clearly suggests that it is the slave labour of one group that provides the pleasure garden of the other. This message is then reinforced by the intrusion into the garden of a woman with a group of dirty barefoot children. Her costume, a plain laced-up dress with a demure collar, sets her apart from the women of pleasure in the garden. Her face is both sad and pleading. Described by the text as the daughter of a worker she appeals to the occupants of the garden to recognise the children as their 'brothers'. Her appeal has a profound effect on Frieder whose privileged position as the son of the master of Metropolis is denoted by his pale aristocratic clothes. He follows her exit and makes his way to the underground areas.

Once underground we see the workers in action, their choreographed rhythmic movements making them at one with the great machine which they tend. We see a worker collapse at his station, the pressure gauge rises and there is an explosion. Workers bodies fly through the air, which is swathed in steam. Out of the steam Frieder's symbolic vision of 'Moloch' – the Canaanite idol to which children were sacrificed – is slowly revealed. The great machine retains the same lines and overall shape but now we see at its centre a huge sphinx-like structure, the entrance to a temple of hell. The workers are now represented as bound slaves being whipped up the steps and thrown into the great demonic mouth at the heart of the machine. Slowly the images of sacrifice fade and we see the great machine once more as the bodies of the dead and wounded are removed on stretchers and the work goes on. It is through the juxtaposition of such images that the tyranny at the heart of Metropolis is made clear. The children who appeared briefly in the pleasure garden will be sacrificed to the great machine to work until they die.

Lang cuts to the image of the skyline in the world above. Again the setting is elaborate and magnificent, dominated by skyscrapers and movement happening on many different planes as cars, trains and planes traverse the city. This futuristic landscape was created in 1926. It is a tribute to the imagination of the set designers that it has been so much copied in films as recent as *Bladerunner* (Scott, USA, 1982), *The Fifth Element* (Besson, France, 1997) and *The Phantom Menace* (Lucas, USA, 1999).

In these opening scenes of *Metropolis* it is the different elements of *mise en scène*, setting, costume, position and movement within the frame and lighting that create very specific meanings. Lang uses settings and contrasts between settings with particular effect: they do more than present us with a landscape of the future, they embody messages and values that enable us to understand and make judgements about the nature of society in Metropolis.

RAIDERS OF THE LOST ARK (SPIELBERG, USA, 1981)

The opening sequence of *Raiders of the Lost Ark* presents us with two distinct settings: the exterior shots in the jungle and the interior shots in the temple where the hero Indiana Jones (played by major league star Harrison Ford) finds the golden Icon. Both settings provide us with information about the hero. In fact this whole opening sequence, a mini-narrative in itself, is designed to introduce Indiana Jones and make us aware of his character.

The opening shot presents us with the image of a mountain, a graphic match of the Paramount logo, which had preceded the moving images. The hero walks into the frame and is positioned so that we see him from behind, silhouetted against the skyline and looking at the mountain which is obviously his destination. His importance is signalled by the fact that he is in the centre of the frame but his identity is withheld from us and we do not see his face. This kind of positioning continues for the first few minutes of the film, creating a mystery and a curiosity in the audience to know who he is. Withholding his face from us forces us to concentrate on the actions we do see and much of his character is established in this way.

We see that he is a leader, knowledgeable and decisive in this jungle terrain, able to interpret signs like the poisoned dart in the tree and weigh up the risks. He is separated from the group through his position (isolated in the lead), his actions (which instigate the actions of the whole group) and his costume, the leather jacket and battered trilby that suggest he is American, in contrast with the bare heads and tattered straw or knitted hats of his followers. His status as leader is further marked out by the fact that he carries no pack of equipment and is not leading a mule like the others. The reluctance with which these others follow him, the apprehension expressed in their faces (which we do see, a further contrast) highlights his determination and lack of fear. He pauses to consult the torn pieces of an ancient-looking map (again our view is restricted to a detail shot showing the hands) and this is the first clear indication that this expedition is some kind of treasure hunt. We have already seen him fearlessly take the lead, undaunted by whatever dangers may be lurking in the jungle. Now in his reading of the map he demonstrates skill and then further proves his bravery/heroic status.

One of his followers, bent on treachery, takes out and cocks his gun behind the hero's back. A shot of Jones' ear indicates super-alert hearing and then he moves swiftly and decisively, spinning round as he cracks his whip with perfect aim to disarm his assailant. His face remains briefly in darkness and then he steps forward into the half-light, finally revealed to us (note the way music and type of shot work in conjunction with the *mise en scène* to create the powerful impact of our first sight of Indiana Jones). Sun-tanned, unshaven, sweat-stained and frowning, he looks mean, tough and competent. We already associate him with bravery and leadership. It is a tremendously dramatic and powerful introduction of character.

All the elements of *mise en scène* – setting, costume, lighting, position and movement within the frame – have been utilised to establish Jones' heroic credentials. So far he has not said a word. Once inside the temple he faces a new series of trials that demonstrate further heroic qualities. It is not just bravery that enables him to successfully navigate the temple, but knowledge. Both these qualities are highlighted by their absence in his sidekick, played by Alfred Molina, whose face and voice express his fear, selfishness and greed. Lighting plays a significant role in the temple. It is important in creating the mood – a certain creepy sense of suspense at what ghoulish horror or device of dark magic might be revealed next – but it also plays a part in the action. Confronted with shafts of light crossing the temple Jones displays his wisdom with his injunction: 'stay out of the light'. He moves his arm into the path of light triggering the death trap – sharpened poles complete with the rotten corpse of his predecessor.

The purpose of this scene is primarily to display his superior wisdom – no one but Dr Jones has ever come out of the temple alive – but the power of light also becomes a theme of the film. It is a beam of light shining through a crystal that reveals the location of the Well of Souls. It is the light of dawn that alerts the Nazis to Indiana's team, enabling them to steal the Ark of the Covenant. Later, when the Ark is opened, the power of God is expressed by light, first beautiful then awesomely destructive.

Costume is equally important in the rest of the film as a means of establishing historical period, cultural background and nationality. Costume in the form of disguise becomes an important feature of the narrative, allowing Indiana Jones to negotiate dangerous territory – we see him at one point in the white turban and flowing robes of the Egyptian, and at another point in an ill-fitting Nazi uniform. Jones' most interesting change of costume, however, has to be the one immediately following the opening sequence of the film. An establishing shot of 'dreaming spires' introduces a new setting – the university campus, and then we see Indiana transformed into his other role. He is no longer a swashbuckling, risk-taking, dare-devil bounty hunter but a respectable academic. The setting (lecture theatre) and props (desk, chalk and blackboard) are important in creating this new image but it is the change in clothes and appearance that has the most significant impact. This scene indicates clearly how important costume can be as an indication of character and the way a character feels about themselves. In his tweed suit Indiana Jones is still knowledgeable but much more diffident and uncertain of himself. When he gets the mission to search for the Ark of the Covenant the qualities we saw in the opening sequence reappear. Significantly, he packs three things in his suitcase: his whip, his gun and his hat. These three items signal clearly to the viewer a return to the characteristics and obsessions of the man of action

Raiders of the Lost Ark is a visually arresting movie. Much of its allure does come from striking images which were taken from and have re-entered the realms of popular culture. A considerable part of the power of these images comes not from what they contain but how they are captured and presented – the realms of cinematography.

Things to watch out for and consider

Setting
- Where/when does the action take place? What details of the setting indicate this?
- How does the setting indicate genre?
- Does the setting indicate mood? If so, how?
- What does the setting suggest about the characters? Their status? Culture? Occupation?

Costume
- Does the costume suggest a certain historical period?
- How does the costume indicate genre?
- What does the costume suggest about the characters' social, cultural, national background?
- Do the characters significantly change their costumes over the course of the film? If so, what does this indicate about their changing feelings/fortunes/status?
- What do the costumes suggest about the way a character feels about themselves? The impression they want to make on others?

Lighting
- Is the lighting high key or low key?
- What kind of mood does the lighting create? Are different lighting techniques being used to create different moods?
- How does the lighting indicate genre?
- Does the colour of the light change for different scenes? If so, to what effect?

Figure expression and movement
- Where are the characters positioned within the frame? Does this reflect their importance? Feelings? Relationships with each other?
- What thoughts, feelings and emotions are evoked by the actors' performances?
- What kinds of movements do we see them engaged in (e.g. fighting/dancing)? What does this convey about them? Their feelings?
- What aspects of figure, expression and movement indicate genre?

2 Cinematography

In the beginning there was just a guy with a camera.
(Michael Chapman)

In Chapter 1 we did not stray from the realms of (admittedly filmed) theatre, but film is a more mediated medium – simply because it is filmed (and projected). This chapter aims to introduce the reader to the unique element of film that is cinematography. The chapter will include an introduction to the basic technical elements of photography and camera placement and movement as well as the types of static and mobile shot used in cinema. The uses of these techniques in order to produce meaning will constitute the central message of this chapter. The dramatic potential of cine-matography will be illustrated by a reading of Chapman's cine-matography in Martin Scorsese's *Raging Bull* (USA, 1980). The relationship between cinematography and editing is discussed via a reading of Orson Welles' *Touch of Evil* (USA, 1958). This chapter concludes with a series of questions designed to help structure cinematographic analysis.

Cinematography, like every activity that contributes to film and film-making, is – of course – a matter of choices. Some of the choices that the cinematographer – or director of photography – has to make, including placing and lighting objects, have already been covered in the *mise en scène* chapter. The difficulty of demar-cation is in itself evidence that the activities involved in film-making do not fit easily into pigeon holes. The difficulty in defining where the cinematographer's 'role' begins and ends is also evidence that film-making is a truly collaborative art. Setting and costume would need to be discussed and planned with production designers, position and framing (as well as lighting, lens and film stock) with the camera operator, logistics with the line producer and lighting choices with all three. Every decision would have to be made with (or possibly by) the director and ultimately the producer.

The simple fact that the camera – as well as the *mise en scène* – needs to be deliberately placed, takes film beyond theatre. As the Hungarian film-maker/theorist Bela Balazs put it: '(theatre) always maintains its action in a spatial continuity, stable distance from the spectator and one unchanged angle'. Whereas in films both the distance and the angle from which we see the action can change. In positioning the camera there are a number of options available to the film-maker. These are:

- camera angle
- camera level
- camera height
- camera distance (from the action).

CAMERA ANGLE

In general, the viewer is used to encountering objects – in particular people – at eye level. Thus the audience feels most comfortable when the material they are viewing has been filmed close to eye-level. Drastic changes from this 'view point' produce powerful psychological effects.

A low angle means that the camera is pointing up. Thus the subject becomes big, possibly threatening but certainly empowered. Several of these monumental shots can be seen in *Citizen Kane* (Welles, USA, 1940) as Welles seeks to make Charles Foster Kane increasingly imposing. A high angle means that the camera is pointing down. Thus the subject becomes small, possibly threatened and clearly drained of power. In *The Truman Show* (Weir, USA, 1998), Truman (Jim Carrey) is positioned as a pawn in a game beyond his understanding by his controllers – and by extension us – frequently watching him from above.

CAMERA LEVEL

Camera level is important too. Day-to-day existence is experienced through two eyes positioned horizontally. We are used to the horizontal view. Breaking that convention by tilting the camera from its horizontal axis ('canting the frame') can have powerful effects. In *The Third Man* (Reed, UK, 1949) Robert Krasker's striking photography is notable not only for its contrasts in tone but also in his use of angles. In the opening scene Holly Martins (played by Joseph Cotton) arrives in Vienna to visit his old friend Harry Lime.

Up to the moment Martins arrives at Lime's apartment the cinematography is unremarkable. As Martins rings Lime's door-bell, the frame is canted and the following scene – in which Martins is led to believe his friend is dead – played out in extreme, mannerist angles. The frame literally shifts to create a feeling of movement – not only of the image but within the narrative too. Martins' seemingly simple choice to join his friend leads him into a complex underworld he cannot possibly deal with.

CAMERA HEIGHT

Whilst the camera is normally at eye-level it is possible to alter the height but keep the angle level. Low-level shots in particular can enhance a feeling of speed in action.

CAMERA DISTANCE

Arguably the most important aspect of camera placement is distance. This term refers to how close or far away the camera is from the action. We call the end result the type of shot, e.g. long shot, mid-shot or close-up (see below for the full list). The camera distance from the action profoundly affects how we respond to the action. It is one of the tools at the film-maker's disposal for creating a 'preferred meaning' (i.e. guiding the audience to respond in a particular way – see Chapters 10 and 11). The type of shot affects the degree of our engagement with the characters and helps us to recognise who/what is the significant aspect of each scene. We engage with the protagonists of a film, for example, not simply because they are cleverer or better looking than everyone else but because they are likely to be accorded the greatest number of close-ups, thus creating a kind of voyeuristic intimacy.

For an understanding of how the choice of shot guides the way in which we read a scene it is useful to look at some examples of early cinema, e.g. *The Great Train Robbery* (Porter, USA, 1903), where the camera remains at a fixed distance from the action (for a reading of *The Great Train Robbery* see Chapter 4). Over time, conventions developed as to how the different types of shot are sequenced to create a scene (see Chapter 3).

Once the camera is placed and positioned the film must be exposed to create pictures. *The shot* is defined as a single, continuously exposed piece of film – however long or short – without any edits or cuts. 'Shot' is the term used in referring to the completed film; the term used whilst filming is 'take'. The 'shot' can be of various types from various distances and angles, and both static and mobile.

Static shots include:
- long shot (often an 'establishing' shot – to set the scene);
- two shot – containing two complete figures and clarifying their spatial relationship;
- full shot – a single figure from head to toe;
- mid-shot – from the waist up;
- close-up – from a 'head and shoulders' to 'chin to eyebrow';
- extreme close-up – tighter than a close-up;
- detail – a close-up of an object.

Mobile shots include:
- zoom (lens)
- pan (camera)
- track (dolly).

Narrative cinema began as filmed theatre. The films were short – up to 10 minutes – and consisted of a single 'tableau'. The action took place before a static camera which had to take in the whole set. The early film-makers directed from behind the camera. They were by nature an adventurous breed. Cameramen all over the world were stretching the boundaries of the form as soon as they started filming. Practically as soon as pictures moved picture-makers were looking at ways to get the camera moving. In the great days of silent cinema an entertainment became an art and the camera as well as the images moved. In France the impressionists used camera movement to express a character's state of mind, e.g. in Epstein's *Cœur Fidèle* (1923), or to highlight drama, e.g. Abel

Gance's *Napoleon* (1927). In the USA camera mobility reached its epitome with the work of Billy Bitzer on such films as *Way Down East* (Griffith, 1920) through to *The Crowd* (Vidor, 1927), photographed by Harry Sharp. The flowing camerawork of late silent cinema came to an end when the needs of sound required the camera to be soundproofed. It could also be argued that the introduction of sound allowed dialogue to take over the major story-telling role that the camera had held in the 1920s. As cinematographer Nestor Almendros put it rather wistfully: 'The early movies seem to be freer . . . The camera was free.'

Shots can be given mobility by shifting the camera on its axes – the pan. The camera can be panned horizontally or vertically to take in a scene or to follow an action. Additional mobility can be produced by actually moving the camera while filming. This can be done on a track – the 'dolly shot' – or, once cameras became light enough, 'hand held'. A modern development that has allowed even more fluidity in 'tracking' has been the 'steadicam' – a counterweighted apparatus which allows the camera to be attached to and move with the operator. Particularly fine use of the 'steadicam' as pursuer/voyeur can be seen in *The Shining* (Kubrick, UK, 1980), *Goodfellas* (Scorsese, USA, 1990) and *Raging Bull* (for a detailed analysis of cinematography in *Raging Bull* see below).

Once the scene is 'set' and lit and framed by the camera, the next decision to make is about the quality and type of image. This decision involves the process of selection of lens and the selection of film stock. The cinematographer must also decide on the amount of light hitting the film (by a combination of exposure time and aperture size). In another example of interconnectivity it is important to note that both these choices must be made in conjunction with decisions about lighting.

CHOICE OF LENS

Lenses are made with various focal lengths, i.e. the distance between the centre of the lens to the point where the light is focused. The focal length of the lens controls the depth and scale of the image. The 'normal' focal length for the lens on a movie camera is 35–50 mm. A short focal length – less than 35 mm – is known as a 'wide-angle' lens. Used in a wide shot this type of lens will produce the 'fish eye' effect of curved edges to the image.

Using this type of lens (but not for a wide shot) with intense lighting it is possible to create deep-focus photography. Thus in *Citizen Kane* the director of photography, Greg Toland, could keep all the planes of action in focus.

A lens with a long focal length – i.e. over 50 mm – is known as a 'telephoto'. The telephoto lens produces a flattened image (accentuating immediacy and speed). In *The Seven Samurai* (Kurosawa, 1954, Japan) Akasaku Nakai used a telephoto in the scene when the peasants go to seek 'hungry Samurai'. Planes of action are tightened to a physically impossible pitch. Moving figures flash past the staring peasants who stand amazed by the hustle and bustle of the town.

Adjusting the focal length whilst filming can be achieved by use of a zoom lens. A zoom from a wide establishing shot to a more or less tight (telephoto) shot or – less usually – vice versa can create a dramatic focus. This technique should not be seen as an alternative to actually moving the camera (dolly). The photographic effect is quite different. In a 'dolly shot' the amount of action within the scene can be decreased (to present a detail) or increased to produce an establishing shot. This latter – rather disconcerting effect – is used with much aplomb by John Alcott on *Barry Lyndon* (Kubrick, UK, 1975). In the 'zoom' the image not only tightens or loosens but the image itself changes too.

Citizen Kane (1941). Reproduced with permission from BFI Stills, Posters and Designs

This effect of tightening the planes of action is unwittingly and all too often used in home videos. In the hands of a director with a cameraman's experience (Nic Roeg) either operating the camera himself, as in *Walkabout* (1971), or with a skilled cinematographer (Anthony Richmond) on *The Man Who Fell to Earth* (1976), the zoom lens can provide rich visual fare. Roeg was able to accentuate elements of the unfamiliar world inhabited by the lost children in *Walkabout*, or the alien in *The Man Who Fell to Earth*, as well as to highlight psychological states.

CHOICE OF FILM STOCK

A sequence from early in *Citizen Kane* (USA, 1941) shows Orson Welles and his cinematographer Greg Toland using a wide range of film stocks and photographic techniques to illustrate the passage of time: the news montage in *Citizen Kane* utilises cinematography as a story-telling tool. Not only was particular stock specifically chosen for particular time periods, the stock was treated and deliberately damaged to add 'authenticity'.

EXPOSURE

The clearest examples of the *use* of exposure are when a director of photography 'breaks the rules', e.g. Vilmos Zsigmond on *McCabe and Mrs Miller* (Altman, 1971). After ten years of low-budget documentaries and exploitation movies Zsigismond was given the opportunity to produce painterly images. Altman required a look that would evoke old photographs. The effect was achieved by 'flashing', using a wider aperture to allow in extra light to 'fog' the film.

Unlike Zsigismond, Toland and a whole line of directors of photography who broke rules by letting in 'too much light', Gordon Willis became known as the 'Prince of Darkness' after *The Godfather* and *The Godfather Part II*. The doomy shadows that dominate those two films were the result of underexposing the film stock. Willis went on to lend his skill with shadow to many of Woody Allen's finest films. With *Annie Hall* (1977), *Manhattan* (1979) and *Purple Rose of Cairo* (1984), Willis showed his ability to utilise both colour and black and white film stock.

COLOUR

The choice between colour and monochrome can be used to make its own points. In the case of *The Wizard of Oz* (Fleming, USA, 1939) the move from a very low-key black and white to vibrant colour signals the move from Kansas into the fantasy of Oz. In Wim Wenders' *Wings of Desire* (Germany, 1989) the 'real' world is seen in black and white by the angel Bruno until he finds love, chooses life and colour returns. In Powell and Pressburger's masterly *A Matter of Life and Death* (UK, 1946) a similar juxtaposition is used to suggest that human life is worth fighting for. In *Schindler's List* (Spielberg, USA, 1993) the monotonous monochrome of the film is broken only twice. As the Jews are rounded up for the ghetto one small girl runs frantically in the crowd. Her movements are highlighted by the fact that her coat is bright red. Her plight personalises the horror of the Holocaust. Late in the film we see the coat again – amongst a pile a corpses.

RAGING BULL (SCORSESE, USA, 1980)

Martin Scorsese's *Raging Bull* (USA, 1980) – photographed by long-time collaborator Michael Chapman – is a master class in the power of cinematography as a story-telling tool. Changes and contrasts in cinematography comment on and progress the narrative.

The film begins with one of the greatest title sequences in cinema history. A caped figure (Jake La Motta, the 'Raging Bull') prowls the boxing ring in slow motion. The background is out of focus, literally smoky, popping with occasional flashes. The whole screen is dominated by the three ropes of the ring nearest to the camera, black and in sharp focus. They are the bars of the bull's cage.

After the opening titles we are offered a brief scene of an ageing La Motta (Robert De Niro) rehearsing for his (awful) night club show. The scene is titled '1964' and followed by La Motta in the ring in 1945 fighting Jimmy Reeves. The initial shots – of La Motta being pummelled by Reeves – are deliberately blurred. As the round ends, the choice of lighting and lens produces an image of

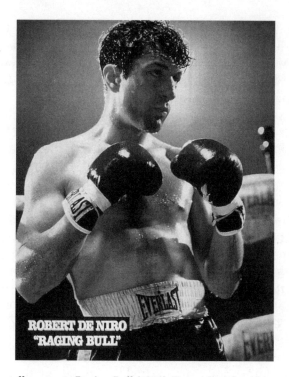

Every picture tells a story, *Raging Bull* (1980). Reproduced with permission from BFI Stills, Posters and Designs

high contrasts and deep focus. In this moment of hiatus the camera tracks in on La Motta to allow the viewer access to events in the corner. Throughout the sequence deep focus and telephoto are juxtaposed to contrast anticipation and explosions of action in and outside of the ring.

The presentation of the defeat of Sugar Ray Robinson in 1943 is more uniform in camera style but contains startling contrasts in speed. The camera is much closer to the action and apparently hand held. The immediacy of the sequence is heightened by the use of a still image on the first knock-down. The following sequence begins in slow motion and builds to furious pace as La Motta moves in for the finish.

In the Robinson rematch the choice of telephoto lens tightens the clinches between the fighters and leaves the backgrounds out of focus. For now only the fighters matter. In the previous scene La Motta has abstained from sex to prepare to fight. La Motta and Robinson are locked together. The voice-over commentary notes that no one else will fight them.

By contrast the non-fight scenes are in rich deep focus. This choice is in itself a tribute to an older style of black and white cinematography and in particular to *On the Waterfront* (Kazan, USA, 1954), the work of Boris Kaufman. The making of *Raging Bull* allowed Scorsese and Chapman to pay homage – and draw connections – to an earlier masterpiece about a boxer and his brother.

Raging Bull also contains sequences from the La Motta home movies. These are the only material in the film presented in colour. The colours are unpleasant and degraded. Like Welles and Toland before him Scorsese had tampered with the stock for dramatic effect. This strategy was certainly an attempt to comment on the unpleasantness underlying La Motta's home life. Scorsese was also making a political point in his campaign for studios to protect their archive prints and for film manufacturers to expend more time and effort on the quality and longevity of their products.

The fights themselves continue to provide Scorsese and Chapman (along with editor Thelma Schoonmaker) with a chance to explore contrasting methods of presentation. The Zivic fight – 1944 – is presented entirely in stills. The Basora fight –1945 – consists of two stills, one blurred punch and a victory pose.

After the deliberately amateurish coverage of the La Motta's wedding the fights continue. Links (trouble at home and in the ring) are suggested. The Kochan fight – 1945 – is presented as a telephoto shot matched to home movies of dancing by the pool. In the two close-up stills of the Edgar fight the Raging Bull really does look enraged. His brother's wedding and the Satterfield fight of 1946 are conjoined in a blur. A montage of family shots ends with a montage of victory shots from the Bell fight of March 1947.

In the Genira fight – retrospectively the Bull's last great fight – the camera work is very fluid and mobile. The Fox bout which follows is a central moment in the film. This is the fight which La Motta threw. The presentation has a slower, dream-like quality which is broken by the stark contrasts and sharp focus of La Motta sobbing in the dressing room.

The story of *Raging Bull* moves forward two years to the comeback bout against Cerdain. The power of La Motta's return to centre stage is accentuated by an extraordinarily long track from the dressing room to the ring. The steadicam – invented after all to be used in sports coverage – is used to breathtaking effect. The viewer is placed in a privileged position to follow the Raging Bull through the crowds to the place where he will redeem his reputation and his own self-worth.

The rematch with Robinson begins as television coverage, then returns to the style of the other Robinson fights. The thirteenth round begins with La Motta rising in slow motion. As the action starts Chapman returns the camera from overcranked (slow motion) to usual speed and thus the action speeds up. La Motta stands apparently beaten yet still calling his opponent to fight. A frenetic sequence of very short shots follows as the final battering begins. Lights flare the lens. The action halts and the camera becomes fluid again. A single gloved hand is caught in the lights. The devastating Robinson punch lands and, accompanied by reaction shots from wife and brother, La Motta's career is ended. The story jumps to 1956 and La Motta sits fat and immobile by his pool.

TOUCH OF EVIL (WELLES, 1958)

The visual power of Scorsese's films comes from a combination of effective use of photographic technique with virtuoso editing (since *Raging Bull*, exclusively the work of Thelma Schoonmaker). The opening of Orson Welles' *Touch of Evil* (USA, 1958) illustrates cinematography in a somewhat purer form. What is immediately noticeable in this famous scene is the lack of editing. The shot lasts over three and half minutes without a cut. Thus all the moving is the result of camera movement and movement within the frame (all done twenty years before the steadicam).

The director of photography, Russell Metty, was a veteran of literally hundreds of films of all genres and styles since 1934. Much like Greg Toland before him, Metty was inspired by Welles to try new ways to stretch the potentialities of film and filming. This experienced old hand was suddenly using a hand-held camera and making a 'New Wave' film before the 'New Wave' had even begun in Europe. For the opening scene Welles pushed his cinematographer and camera operator to the ultimate mobile shot: legend has it as the longest single crane shot in cinema history.

The scene/shot begins unusually with a close-up. Attention is immediately grabbed not only by the shock of beginning with a detail rather than an establishing shot but also because the 'detail' is a bomb. The figure holding the bomb swings round as voices approach. So does the camera. As the bomber runs the camera sweeps into fluid motion. Once the bomb is placed in the car the camera 'takes off' to survey the scene. The camera precedes rather than tracks the car. When the car stops the camera changes direction to track a walking couple, fluidly swooping down to proceed with them through the streets. The car passes between the camera and the couple but continues untracked out of frame. Deep-focus photography allows Welles to show us several groups of people crossing the frame. This photographic technique along with a highly mobile camera allows Welles to elongate the scene and build tension. This approach is a direct opposite of the cinematography which created such a sense of excitement in the street scene in *The Seven Samurai*. The walking couple (central characters played by Charlton Heston and Janet Leigh) and the couple in the car come to a halt together at the customs post. The camera rests too. The camera holds its position as the couple circle the car. It moves again as the car moves – but follows Heston and Leigh. The shot ends with the two stars perfectly centred in the frame as they kiss – and the bomb explodes off screen. The difficulty of constructing this shot can be seen by the sunrise clearly in evidence at the end of the shot.

The opening scene of Robert Altman's *The Player* (USA, 1992) is a play on this 'longest take'. As the mobile camera of Jean Lepine roams around a studio lot various 'types' go about their business. One character even refers to the original model: 'my old man was key grip on that shoot'. It is worth noting that both the original and the parody are title sequences. Is it possible that we cannot handle such long shots without the distraction of text? These 'unedited' shots are legendary because they are so unusual. The next chapter explores the basic rules of telling stories by putting shots together.

Things to watch out for and consider

Camera placement
- Where is the camera positioned in relation to the action (i.e. long shot, close-up)? What is the function and effect of this position (e.g. to establish/to draw attention to a character/detail)?
- Is the camera angle straight on (most shots), high or low? What is the function and effect of different camera angles?
- Is the shot level (most shots) or canted? What is the function and effect of different camera levels?

- Does the camera height remain (roughly) at eye-level (most shots) or do we see shots positioned from different heights? What is the function and effect of positioning the camera at different heights?

Camera mobility
- Is the camera static or mobile? What is the function and effect of a static camera?
- If the camera is moving, what different types of mobile shot do we see (i.e. pan, track, dolly)? What is the function and effect of these different types of mobile shot?

Film stock
- Is the film shot in black and white or colour film stock or a combination of both?
- What do you consider to be the film-maker's likely reasons for choosing the type(s) of film stock? What is the effect of the particular type of film stock? What is the effect of using a combination of different types/qualities of film stock?

Choice of lens
- Are the shots being filmed with a standard, wide-angle or telephoto lens? Does the cinematographer utilise a zoom?
- What is the function and effect of these different types of lens?

Cinematography is a primary tool with which the film-maker can guide the way in which the viewer responds to the *mise en scène*. Consider whether the film-maker is using the cinematography to close down the number of ways in which a scene can be interpreted (a relatively closed text) or to open up the number of ways in which a scene can be interpreted (a more open text), e.g. using a wide-angle lens to film a scene in deep focus opens up the options for the spectator (we can choose which aspect of the action to look at).

3 Editing

Film art begins from the moment when the director begins to combine and join together the various pieces of film.

(Lev Kuleshov, 1921)

Kuleshov's epithet on the central importance of the edit comes from his opening lecture to students at the First State Film School in Moscow. The film-maker, having placed the material (*mise en scène*) and chosen how to frame and film it (cinematography) must now make a final set of decisions around the issues of how that material is put together (usually to tell coherent stories): editing. It is important to note at this point that our separation out of the film-making process is a gross simplification made to aid analysis. The choices involved in *mise en scène* and cinematography, and in all likelihood editing too, will take place at the same time and all affect each other.

Whilst it remains arguable as to whether editing is the most important element in film-making, it is true to say that it is that most quintessentially cinematic element of cinema (writing in movement).

This chapter introduces the reader to the various methods of joining shots and the techniques of continuity. Central to this chapter will be a discussion of the relationship between editing and storytelling. The power of editing to tell stories and elicit responses from audiences will be illustrated by close readings of two of the iconographic moments in film history: the 'Potemkin Steps' sequence from *Battleship Potemkin* (Eisenstein, 1926) and the shower scene from *Psycho* (Hitchcock, 1960). The chapter concludes with a series of questions designed to aid the analysis of editing.

As we saw in the previous chapter, movies are made up of

shots. Almost all shots contain movement (within, in and out of frame) and some shots move in themselves (tracking, dolly, crane). All shots are given movement by the way they are combined. On the editing table the shots are selected and ordered to create a narrative structure and, hopefully, aesthetic interest.

Editing film enables the film-maker to take liberties with the space–time continuum. Real life and theatre can only happen in real time and real space. Editing allows us to both protract and contract real time, and to make spatial leaps approaching the speed of light. For example: the men are about to be shot, the pram is going down the steps, a time bomb is ticking; meanwhile . . . back at the ranch . . . This enablement gives a spatial omnipresence and omniscience (usually associated with narrators rather than readers) and a sense of empowerment (although it is an illusion).

If you pause to think about it, films are made up of hundreds of fragments (shots) stuck together most frequently by the straight cut, which means that the images we are viewing are constantly and instantaneously changing. It ought to be disorientating and confusing and yet it's not. As viewers we are usually not conscious of the fragmentary nature of film at all. There are two reasons for this:

- the rules of continuity editing;
- the cine-literacy of viewers.

The earliest films did not involve editing. The entire film would consist of one shot. The camera was set up in one position and the action would unfold before it in a continuous take. Sometimes film-makers would make a series of shots of the same subject but these were treated as separate films. Once it became possible to create longer films by editing shots together the artistic and narrative possibilities for film expanded enormously.

Editing allows film-makers to exercise control over space, time, narrative structure, the rhythm of the film and the visual impact that can be created from the juxtaposition of two shots. But at the same time editing presents the film-maker with problems. It fragments the film. Early film-makers soon discovered that this could cause confusion unless the spectator understood how the shots were related to each other in terms of time and space. Is time continuing without interruption or has some time been skipped? Are we still seeing the same space or have we moved to a new location? The challenge to film-makers is to find a way of overcoming these potential areas of confusion by constantly signalling to the viewer where and when the action is taking place – in other words to make the relationship between shots clear and easy to follow.

When we look at editing there are a number of different areas we can focus on, all of which involve choices by the film-maker:

- editing style
- editing and space
- editing and time
- editing and rhythm
- matching
- graphic matching
- compilation shots
- montage
- editing and sound.

EDITING STYLE

How has each shot been joined to the next? The options are:

- the straight cut – which gives an instantaneous jump from one image to the next;
- the fade – where the screen fades to black;
- the dissolve – where one image is slowly brought in beneath another one;
- the wipe – where the new image pushes the old one off the screen to indicate that a sequence has finished and the story is moving to a different field of action;
- the iris – where the shutter of the lens is closed in to form a smaller and smaller circular picture (or the reverse where the shutter of the lens is opened out).

Over time, conventions developed as to which style of editing to use in different situations. Most film narratives can be broken down into scenes or sequences where the location is first established and then the action develops before the film moves on to a new scene. Straight cuts are likely to be used within a scene. Breaks between scenes are often marked with a fade to indicate the close of one sphere of action and the opening of the next one. (Fading to black gives us a more decisive break than a straight cut.) A flashback or a dream sequence is likely to be signalled by a dissolve or fade, often on the face of the character whose flashback we are about to witness. The wipe, originally popular in the serials of the 1930s and 1940s, is rarely used nowadays except by George Lucas in the *Star Wars* films to indicate that a sequence has finished and the story is moving to a different field of action.

EDITING AND SPACE

Editing permits the film-maker to move between one location and another, in fact to relate any two points in space. Most films utilise different settings, even if this is limited to interior and exterior shots of a house. If the film is going to move between different spaces it becomes really important to signal to the viewer where the action takes place and when the location changes. Just relying on the background to look roughly the same isn't enough, as a location will look completely different according to the position of the camera. It is also necessary to maintain consistency of screen direction. If you film a character walking down a road from one pavement, and then cut to a shot of them walking down the road filmed from the opposite pavement, it will look as if they have turned around and started walking the other way.

Cross-cutting is the technique of cutting between two sequences that are occurring at the same time but in different locations. This technique was developed by the great American pioneer D. W. Griffith. The effect of cross-cutting is usually to create suspense and speed up the narrative, so it is often used in Westerns, thrillers and gangster movies. Particular film-makers, e.g. Francis Ford Coppola in his *Godfather* films, have developed the cross-cut into a visual signature.

EDITING AND TIME

Film involves time as well as space. Editing gives the film-maker the option of choosing the order in which we see events. Most film narratives are linear, which means that events move forward through time in a chronological order. The exception is the use of flashbacks which show scenes from an earlier time than the rest of the story.

Most films don't happen in real time. In the space of two hours a story that takes days, weeks or months can be conveyed. This means that chunks of time are being skipped and the narrative is moving on to 'later that day', six months, later, etc. These ellipses need to be signalled to the viewers so that they can follow events. Signalling methods include captions and voice-overs, wipes, the fade to black, the cross-fade and the dissolve.

EDITING AND RHYTHM

How long does each shot last? It could be a few seconds or it could be a few minutes. The length of each shot will determine the pace of the action (including changes of pace) and will affect the mood of what is taking place on screen. Extreme examples of long duration of shot include the ending of *The Third Man* (Reed, UK, 1949), where time seems to stand still as Anna strides past the waiting Holly Martins. Conversely, time itself speeds up by shortening the duration of shots at the end of *The Man With the Movie Camera* (Vertov, USSR, 1929).

MATCHING

The relationship between shots can be clarified if shots are matched according to action, subject, or subject matter. Match cutting ensures that there is a spatial–visual logic between the differently positioned shots within a scene. In a typical Western shoot-out a shot can go from a long shot of both protagonists via a cut to a medium close-up of one of the protagonists. The cut matches the two shots and is consistent with the action.

Matching is used extensively within scenes to seamlessly knit the action together but can also be used between scenes to bridge the action and make a connection for the viewer. A fairly typical device to indicate a connection between two characters is to match their actions. For example, a shot could show us one character looking at her alarm clock in the middle of the night. A cut could then show an alarm clock going off, indicating morning, but this time we see a different character in a different room switch it off. Thus we are encouraged to link these two characters.

Matching on action can often be used to smooth the transition between one period of time and another. If you want to suggest that years have passed and a character has grown from child to adulthood you can show the child performing some action, for example painting at an easel, dancing a particular dance, and then cut to a shot of the adult performing the same action. The abrupt nature of the ellipses is therefore made coherent to the viewer who understands that it is the same character grown up. Recent Disney films, e.g. *The Lion King* (1994) and *Tarzan* (1998) are particularly fond of this technique.

GRAPHIC MATCHING

This involves a smooth visual transfer (not an *absolute* match) from one shot to the next. The image doesn't have to be the same but it could have the same shape, the same patterns of light and dark areas, or the same positioning of objects/characters within the frame. *Schindler's List* (Spielberg, 1993) opens with the contemporary celebration of Passover. As the ceremonial candles burn out, smoke spirals upwards. This smoke signal is cut to the smoke from a train – at the beginning of the Holocaust.

COMPILATION SHOTS

This is the term used to describe a series of shots spliced together to give a quick impression of a place, e.g. the opening of *The Maltese Falcon* (Huston, USA, 1941) uses a brief compilation sequence of San Francisco to establish the city. Alternatively, a compilation sequence can be used to give a quick impression of a situation, e.g. police arriving at a murder scene: shots of the crowd, journalists, detectives, the corpse, or a story moving on, e.g. the 'montage' sequences in *Summer of Sam* (Lee, USA, 1999).

MONTAGE

A rapid succession of shots juxtaposing images so that the overall effect is greater than the individual parts (for a more detailed discussion of montage see the second half of this chapter).

EDITING AND SOUND

One of the ways in which a film-maker can minimise the fragmentary nature of film is to use sound to provide continuity from one shot to the next. The images might frequently change but they can be connected by a musical score that has the effect of knitting the shots together into a scene or sequence. Another way of using sound to the same effect is through sound bridges. Diegetic sound (sound which belongs in the world of the film, e.g. dialogue or music that a character is playing) continues from one shot into the next. In the opening scene of *Raging Bull* Jake La Motta ends his monologue with 'That's entertainment.' This line is repeated and becomes an ironic comment on the next image we see: the younger La Motta being beaten in the ring. In an early scene from Charles' life in *Citizen Kane* the line 'Merry Christmas . . .' is followed by 'Happy New Year', but said ten years later.

CONTINUITY EDITING

By 1917 in Hollywood a series of techniques to make the connections between shots clear and coherent had been developed – this became known as the continuity editing system. It is designed to make the fragments of film knit together invisibly and coherently so that the viewer understands the action and is not disrupted by the changes from one shot to the next. It is interesting to note that whilst it is called continuity editing many of the rules are about cinematography – the position of the camera and the type of shot being of paramount importance. Continuity editing is about getting the right kinds of shots that can be edited together in such a way as to be coherent to the viewer – more evidence of the collaborative interdependent nature of the medium, no single aspect is really separate from another.

THE ELEMENTS OF CONTINUITY EDITING

- the axis of action or the 180-degree rule
- the 30-degree rule
- the establishing shot
- shot/reverse shot
- eye-line matching
- matching on action
- re-establishing shot

The 180-degree rule

'The axis of action' is the term used to describe an imaginary (straight) line drawn between protagonists in a scene. The camera position is planned around this line. The purpose of the 180-degree rule is to ensure spatial continuity – to make sure that the viewer understands the overall space within which the action takes place and to maintain consistency of screen direction. The basic rule for film-makers is to plan the *mise en scène* around this imaginary line and then to position the camera so that it never crosses the line. (It is possible to cross the line with a moving camera but not with a cut from one side of the line to another.) If the camera crosses the line the effect will be disorientating, not only will the background change but screen direction will be reversed.

A typical sequence might read thus: shot 1 might be a long shot of two characters walking towards each other down a street and shot 2 might be a medium close-up of one of these characters. If both these shots are filmed from the same side of the line, the second shot will show the single character walking in the same direction as before (say from left to right). The viewer will assume that this shot continues from the previous one and the two characters are still approaching each other. If, however, the axis of action has been crossed by placing the camera on the opposite side of the street to film shot 2, screen direction will be reversed and the single character will now be walking from the right side of the screen to the left. It will look to the viewer as if he has changed his mind and turned around.

By following the 180-degree rule the film-maker ensures some common space from shot to shot, orientating the viewer in the scene. Once the scene is finished a new axis of action is established to begin the next scene.

The 30-degree rule

This rule states that between shots the camera position must change by at least 30 degrees in order to avoid a jump cut. If the camera position obeys the 30-degree rule then the viewer will accept that they are viewing the scene from a new point of view. If the camera position is changed by less than 30 degrees the cut will appear startlingly obvious as the whole scene will appear to jump. (More than 30 degrees and it looks like you have moved to a new vantage point, less than 30 degrees and it looks like the whole world has moved.) Some film-makers choose deliberately to use the jump cut for its startling effect, e.g. Jean Luc Godard in *Breathless* (France, 1959) but it would be totally out of place in the classic realist tradition of Hollywood, which seeks to efface the editing process and join the narrative seamlessly.

The establishing shot

In the continuity system a scene will start with an establishing shot, which is a long shot delineating the overall space in which the scene is to take place. If the scene were to take place in a bar, for example, an establishing shot would show the whole of the bar before the scene is broken down into closer shots that might focus in on the central characters at a particular table. This ensures that the viewer clearly understands where the action takes place.

Shot/reverse shot

Once the space has been established (see above) and an axis of action created, closer shots of the characters are possible. Conversation between characters is usually presented using a shot/reverse shot, sometimes called an over-the-shoulder shot because the shoulder of one character is often within the frame. The second shot is not literally the reverse of the first (this would mean crossing the line): the camera is in fact at the opposite end of the axis of action.

Eye-line matching

This is where the first shot shows a character looking off screen at something and the second shot shows the object/character being looked at (from the first character's point of view). Both shot/reverse shot and eye-line matching ensure that even if the characters are not in the frame together we are sure of their where-abouts.

Matching on action

Another way of moving the camera between cuts but still ensuring spatial continuity is to match the cuts on action. The first shot might show a character starting to walk across the room. The second shot shows the same character arriving at the other side of the room. The middle part has been cut out but continuity is maintained because the action is consistent.

Re-establishing shot

Once a scene has progressed for a while with shot/reverse shot showing the characters in close-up a re-establishing shot, which is a return to a long shot of the overall space, re-orientates the viewer into the scene.

The overall purpose of continuity editing is to present time and space in an unproblematic and coherent manner. Beginnings and endings of a scene are clearly demarcated. Shots throughout a scene orient the viewer in time and space and a scene ends clearly indicating where the narrative will get picked up in the next scene. Abrupt changes of pace are avoided. This doesn't mean that the pace can't change, but it will do so steadily.

Two sequences can furnish us with examples of what can be achieved – and with what different dramatic effects – by editing. The opening sequences of *To Have and Have Not* (Hawks, USA, 1944) and *Breathless* (Godard, France, 1959) are justly admired for their effectiveness.

The opening shot of the *To Have and Have Not* (shot 1) presents us with the image of a map of the Caribbean. The camera slowly tracks closer and text anchoring the image explains that we are in 'Martinique in the summer of 1940 shortly after the fall of France'. Thus, in accordance with the continuity system, the scene is being established in terms of both time and space. Further text then gives us the specific location: 'Fort De France' and the film then cuts to shot 2, an establishing shot of a busy port. Harry Morgan (played by Humphrey Bogart) walks into the centre of the frame and up to the police navigation office window. He stops and says 'morning'. The film cuts to shot 3, a two-shot of Morgan and the police navigation officer. The cut is bridged by the dialogue as the officer responds 'Good morning Captain Morgan'. They are positioned in this shot so that a clear axis of action is established between the two characters whose conversation is then edited using shot/reverse shot (shots 3, 4 and 5).

As their conversation concludes, Bogart walks away from the window and the camera pans round as he walks down the dock away from and with his back to the camera. The film then cuts to shot 6; the camera is now on the other side of the action so that Bogart is walking towards rather than away from it. The potentially abrupt nature of this cut is masked by the match on action. In this brief opening sequence it is possible to see how the continuity system achieves smoothness. The transitions between shots are matched on action or bridged using sound. The system also creates a sense of coherence. The viewer is clear about where and when the action takes place through the use of the initial text and the way the shots are sequenced (establishing shot first, before the camera moves closer to the action to reveal the characters).

In this sequence the continuity system can be seen as a functional process. The system functions in establishing where and when the action takes place and defining the way the shots are ordered to make up the scene (establishing shot, dialogue presented by shot/reverse shot).

Breathless provides us with a complete contrast to *To Have and Have Not* (or indeed any classic Hollywood film) as Godard abandons the conventions of film storytelling made so popular by Hollywood in favour of a more experimental style. It's not that he doesn't know what the rules are but that he consciously chooses to break them.

The very first shot of the film indicates a departure from the continuity system as we see a close-up instead of the usual long shot to establish where the action is taking place. This close-up is of a newspaper ad. We see a girl, dressed briefly in frilled pants and a skimpy top, standing in a provocative pose. We hear a voice proclaiming 'so I'm a son of a bitch' but the connection between words and image is not clear – we cannot see a speaker. The camera pans up and we see the character of Michel (played by Jean-Paul Belmondo), hat tilted over his forehead, cigarette between his lips. He runs his thumb over his lips in a homage to Bogart (a visual reference to Hollywood cinema that will be developed as the film progresses). Michel looks off-screen right, following the convention of the eyeline match, and we cut to shot 2. At this point we begin to feel the consequence of the lack of establishing shots. We see a mid-shot of a girl against the backdrop of some city street. It is not clear if she is in the same scene as Michel or not. We cannot work it out from the setting. We have not seen enough of the overall space to orientate ourselves into the scene. Further confusion is added because she is looking off-screen right – the same direction as Michel in the previous scene. If this is an eye-line match we would expect her to be looking off-screen left as if back towards him. She turns her head to look at something off-screen left then back off-screen right and nods. It is not clear with any of these movements what/who she is looking at.

Shots 3 and 4 repeat the pattern of cutting between Michel and the girl which in itself invites us to link them, but screen direction still remains inconsistent with the coventions of the eye-line match. Shot 5 shows a couple getting out of the car. Is this what she has been looking at? Shot 6 shows Michel again looking off-screen left and then turning to look off-screen right. Shot 7 shows the girl nodding and waving. We now see that she is behind the couple leaving the car so we know at least that they are in the same scene together. Shot 8 shows Michel looking off-screen right and folding up his newspaper. Shot 9 shows boats on water, one of which is pulling in to dock – again the lack of an original establishing shot makes this potentially confusing until the camera pans round to show the girl. Shot 10 shows Michel hot-wiring the car. Shot 11 shows the girl running towards something. Shot 12 shows Michel getting into the car. Shot 13 shows the girl appearing and asking to go with him.

By the time we get to the end of this scene it is possible to work out the sequence of events, but by abandoning the continuity editing system Godard forces the spectator to work hard at making sense of the relationship between shots. What is the effect of this on the spectator? The experience is a disorientating one which illustrates a number of things about how much as spectators we are used to having films constructed in a particular way. Whether we have studied film or not we are all cine-literate, we know how to read films (that is make sense of them) but this ability is based on our knowledge of the conventions of film storytelling developed in Hollywood in the studio era. We expect, without being aware of the expectation, to have scenes constructed according to the rules of continuity and for motivation to be clear (see cause and effect relationship between events in Chapter 4). In other words, we expect the film-maker to guide us in our reading of a scene by making space and time comprehensible, by making the relationship between shots clear and by highlighting important or significant moments through the cinematography (e.g. close-ups on important characters and reactions). When a film-maker breaks away from these conventions the effect might be confusing initially but is ultimately provocative, forcing the spectator to think.

Critics who like to see cinema as an intelligent art form, demanding of spectators more than passive engagement, often point to the (film-making and theoretical) work of Sergei M. Eisenstein (1898–1948) as a model.

Eisenstein's fundamental contribution to film-making technique was seeing that the shot was only the start of the film: the building block from which the actual film was assembled. The film was really made on the editing table. The edit itself became the essence of the art form.

In 1918 Sergei Eisenstein joined the 'red' side in the civil war sweeping Russia. After victory in the war he joined the Proletkult theatre. Thus his public career began in theatre. He was enlightened as to the power of cinema by his friend Esfir Shub, who was editing western films for the Soviet authorities. Eisenstein experimented with film inserts in stage plays before changing his career.

He wrote in *Lef*, no. 3, 1923 of 'the montage of attractions' as a new concept: 'a free montage with arbitrarily chosen independent (of both the particular composition and any thematic connection with the actors) effects (attractions) but with the precise aim of specific thematic effect.'

There remains a controversy about who – if anybody –

deserves the credit for this discovery. Eisenstein certainly did not invent editing. For that we must return practically to the beginnings of cinema and the work of Georges Melies. It was Melies (a professional magician) who first produced startling transitions by editing shots together. Eisenstein could not claim to have invented editing as a storytelling medium – juxtaposing action from different times and places – either. That honour should probably go to Edwin S. Porter's *The Great Train Robbery* (1903). The art of storytelling in pictures had already reached the highest levels of sophistication, with D. W. Griffith, a decade before Eisenstein ever filmed anything.

Eisenstein was not even the first film-maker/theorist to decide that editing was the pre-eminent element of film language. That honour is best claimed by Lev Kuleshov. At the first state film school in Moscow Kuleshov worked without film stock. He therefore conducted experiments with short sequences of old stock. A single shot of the great Russian actor Mozzhukin was combined with various other shots: a bowl of soup, a woman undressing, a dead baby. The combination produced meaning: hunger, lust, grief. Thus Kuleshov would claim (1921): 'Film art begins from the moment when the director begins to combine and join together the various pieces of film.'

However, Eisenstein is seen as the father of *montage* because he is its chief theorist. *Montage* is a vital and sophisticated form of editing in which the shots, frequently fairly short ones, are edited together in such a way that the finished sequence has an artistic effect greater than the sum of its component parts. It is the ordering, sequence and juxtaposition of the individual shots which creates the vital impact of montage.

Eisenstein's montage aimed to go beyond Kuleshov's 'A + B = A/B' where two elements were combined to produce a composite image. A + B could create C, a new meaning. A and B can be seemingly entirely unrelated in subject matter. C is the implied meaning, which is never actually shown.

Eisenstein was also an overtly political film-maker. His slogan became: 'ART THROUGH REVOLUTION: REVOLUTION THROUGH ART'. His first three feature films were a trilogy. In *Strike* (1924) he portrayed revolutionary consciousness in need of leadership. *Battleship Potemkin* (1925) was based on an incident from the failed revolution of 1905. *October* (1927) was the filmic version of the successful revolution of 1917. All three are brilliant, as in both very clever and shining formal pieces of film-making.

BATTLESHIP POTEMKIN (EISENSTEIN, 1925)

Battleship Potemkin has its claims to be 'the greatest film ever made'. The 'Odessa steps' sequence is certainly one of the most celebrated (and copied) sequences in the history of film-making. The good people of Odessa have been fêting the sailors who have risen against their cruel officers. A holiday mood has enveloped the crowd on the steps leading to the harbour.

The energising effect of the following sequence comes not from the relentless downward motion or the short shot lengths. Eisenstein actually utilises many screen directions within a basically downward sweep. In addition there are a number of rather long shots, e.g. the central moment when the mother walks *up* the steps with her injured child.

Here is Eisenstein's own description of 'the steps' – from (*Battleship Potemkin*, trans. G. Aitken (1968), p 14):

> movement – is used to express mounting emotional intensity.
>
> Firstly there are close-ups of human figures rushing chaotically. Then long shots of the same scene. (Eisenstein is deliberately breaking with the theatrical practice of establishing the scene and then focusing on detail.) The chaotic movement (obviously very carefully cut together) is next superseded by shots showing the feet of soldiers as they march rhythmically down the steps.
>
> Tempo increases. Rhythm accelerates.
>
> And then, as the downward movement reaches its culmination, the movement is suddenly reversed, instead of the headlong rush of the crowd down the steps we see a solitary figure of a mother carrying her dead son, slowly and solemnly going up the steps.

Rhythm is the key to editing, whether performed by a formalist master like Eisenstein or a jobbing assistant on a music video. Because the great Soviet director has such a clear sense of rhythm built into this sequence he can insert images that appear to be unconnected, e.g. members of the crowd filling the frame or moving in contrapuntal directions. He can also repeat sequences, e.g. the mother falling as the pram teeters on the step, the pram's progress downwards and the final flourish of the Cossack officer's sword slash. It must always be remembered that the aim of all this technique is to heighten the drama: 'a free montage . . . with the precise aim of specific thematic effect'.

The coda to this section shows the power of associative montage and Eisenstein at his imaginative best. The guns of the battleship make their reply to the barbarity. They shell 'Odessa Theatre – headquarters of the generals'. Amidst shots of the destruction we see architectural details: cherubs appear to observe the destruction. The stone lion – lying, sitting, standing – is edited in sequence to produce an ideogram of a lion – the people – rising in defiance.

PSYCHO (HITCHCOCK, 1960)

Alfred Hitchcock – unlike Eisenstein – was not inclined to issue manifestos or engage in theoretical debates. In addition his craft lay in trying to hide his techniques in order to increase the impact of his effects. His mastery can be seen in that famous shower scene – including the build up and 'warm down'. Hitchcock (and editor George Tomasini) performs like a great athlete – but does not want to destroy the fabric of the film.

After their heavily significant conversation about traps Norman (Anthony Perkins) leaves Marion (Janet Leigh). He spies on her briefly through a hole in the wall and then returns to the Bates house. He is seen from behind slouching resignedly around the ground floor. The action returns to the interior of Marion's cabin and we see a mid-shot (shot 1) of her sitting at a desk in her dressing-gown, writing in a notebook. Following the rules of continuity this is then matched with the next shot (shot 2), a detail shot of the notebook showing her calculations. Shot 3 (lasting almost 28 seconds) shows her tear up the page from the notebook and deliberate about how to dispose of it. She gets up and walks to the bathroom and the camera pans to follow her and then cuts to a shot of her through the bathroom door (shot 4). Shot 5 is a detail shot of her flushing the torn pieces of paper down the toilet. Shots 6–8 show her getting in to the shower. We then see a sequence of 9 shots (shots 9–18) showing her showering from various camera positions. Thus in the scene described so far the rules of continuity are adhered to so that the narrative is clear and easy to follow. The pace is measured with lengthy shots being used to suggest that the character is thinking.

It's all in the cutting, *Psycho* (1960). Reproduced courtesy of The Academy of Motion Picture Arts and Sciences

As Marion starts her shower the pace accelerates and remains measured with each shot lasting 4–5 seconds – until shot 18. Here we see Marion showering but through the curtain we see the bathroom door open and a shadowy figure appears. Marion remains oblivious. Hitchcock refrains from cutting to focus on the figure entering the bathroom. Instead the camera tracks slowly closer to the curtain until Marion disappears from view and the shadowy threat is centre frame. At this point the curtain is pulled back to the accompaniment of the sudden dramatic violin sounds and we see a figure in darkness raising a knife into the air. This one shot lasts for 17 seconds and takes us from the peaceful solitude of Marion's shower through rising tension to the moment of crisis.

The abrupt and dramatic action of pulling back the curtain signals the moment of change – in action, in pace, in technique and in sound. The next 29 shots take place in just 20 seconds. Many of them obviously last for less than a second. This tremendously dramatic change in pace effectively conveys the frenzy of the attack and Marion's panic as she tries to protect herself from the assault. The brutality is made more vivid by the way that the speed of the edits matches the speed of the knife strokes raining down on her.

Or so it seems. What do we actually see? – shots of Marion's screaming face, shots of a silhouetted figure raising a knife, shots of the arm and knife plunging downwards, a shot of her belly with the blade of the knife approaching, a shot of her feet with water and blood beginning to splash round them. We do not see her being stabbed (unlike in the remake (Van Sant, USA, 1998) which is more graphic in its portrayal). Hitchcock has moved from the continuity technique to associative montage. A series of images are sequenced in such a way that we infer something that has not been shown.

Sound is particularly effective in this scene. The shrieking staccato sound of the violins emulates the stabbing motion dramatically enhancing the sense and horror of what is taking place. The change in music to much slower deeper notes indicates the next change in pace. After the murderer's exit we see a slow detail shot of Marion's hand begin to slide down the tiled wall of the shower. The next eight shots, which take us to the end of the shower scene with Marion lying static and staring on the floor, take over 80 seconds. Hitchcock has finished his little 'joke' – killing off the star less than halfway through the film. Now he is ready to get on with the main narrative of the picture. In the next chapter we will look at strategies for constructing complete narratives.

Things to watch out for and consider

- What method of joining shots has the film-maker utilised within scenes? Between scenes?
- Is the pace of the editing measured and even or does the film-maker employ abrupt changes of pace? What is the function and effect of the pace and/or changes in pace?
- How are shots within and between sequences matched?
- Are sequences constructed in a continuous or discontinuous manner? How is this achieved and to what effect?
- Does the film-maker utilise montage or compilation sequences? To what effect?
- Does the film-maker utilise cross-cutting? To what effect?
- How and to what effect are editing and sound being used in conjunction with each other?

4 The development of narrative

A story should have a beginning, a middle and an end . . . but not necessarily in that order.

(Jean Luc Godard)

Most film-making actually begins with a story or script. Almost all of the cinema material exhibited to a mainstream audience is thoroughly grounded in storytelling. Even such a distinguished cinematographer as James Wong Howe (*King's Row* (Wood, 1942) and *The Sweet Smell of Success* (MacKendrick, 1957)) admits: 'When you make a movie you got to have a story.' This chapter constitutes a history of storytelling in film. It also allows the student to critically evaluate theories of narratology. An analysis of the use of sound and music in the construction and continuity of narrative is included in this chapter. This chapter concludes with a series of questions designed to help structure analysis of narrative.

Film-makers talk about stories and scripts. Film theorists talk about narrative. Essentially they are talking about the same thing but using different words to do it. We can clarify the situation with a definition. David Bordwell and Kristin Thompson *Film Art: an introduction* (p. 55) define narrative as 'a chain of events in cause–effect relationship occurring in time and space'. Timothy Corrigan in *A Short Guide to Writing about Film* (pp. 36–70) identifies two principle components in a narrative:

- the story is all the events that are presented to us or that we can infer have happened;
- the plot is the arrangement of those events in a certain order or structure.

The study of a film's narrative then is both the study of its story and also the study of how the story is told: by what means (*mise en scène*, cinematography, editing and sound) and in what order (structure).

CLASSIC NARRATIVE CINEMA/ CLASSIC HOLLYWOOD NARRATIVE

This refers to the narrative tradition that dominated Hollywood from the 1930s to the 1960s but which also pervaded western cinema (see Chapter 5). Most contemporary mainstream cinema will share many elements of the classic Hollywood narrative, which is constructed around the following principles:

* cinematic style focuses on creating verisimilitude;
* events follow the basic structure of order/disorder/order restored;
* the narrative is linear;
* events are linked by cause and effect;
* the plot is character-led, thus the narrative is psychologically (and individually) motivated – usually towards the attainment of some goal or desire;
* the role of the hero is central;
* the narrative has closure.

CINEMATIC STYLE AND VERISIMILITUDE

This means that all aspects of the *mise en scène*, cinematography, editing and sound are geared towards creating an appearance of reality encouraging the spectator to forget that the film is constructed and performed and lose themselves in the story. Arguably the most potentially distracting elements of film language are cinematography and editing, which by constantly changing the image, camera position and point of view have the capacity to draw attention to themselves and to the nature of film (thus inhibiting the spectator's ability to forget the medium and be absorbed in the story). Continuity editing (see previous chapter) was developed to overcome these problems and create a smooth and realistic narrative experience. By the 1930s the system was well polished and effective, more importantly it was (and is) what viewers expected, thus further ensuring its effectiveness.

STRUCTURE

The classic Hollywood narrative starts with a state of order or equilibrium. A crisis occurs in the early part of the film which disrupts this initial state of order. The body of the film is concerned with the consequences and effects of the initial crisis. At the end of the film a new order is established. Simply put, the film has a beginning, middle and end.

LINEAR NARRATIVE

Linearity in narrative means quite simply that time runs forward chronologically. The beginning, middle and end (and all points between) occur *in that order*. Our check list of narrative principles may seem rather pat and unlike the messiness of real life but the forward movement of time is the perception that all viewers feel most comfortable with. In *Stagecoach* (Ford, USA, 1939) periods of time – including night – may be removed for the comfort of the viewer but there is no doubt that the order of events shown are the order they would occur in.

In the classic narrative the only common exception to this linearity is the use of flashbacks. These flashbacks must be very clearly signalled. The narrative of *Casablanca* (Curtiz, USA, 1940) is enriched, and to some extent explained, by a flashback to the Paris which Rick and Ilsa will 'always have'.

The sequence begins with Rick in his closed bar, drinking and showing emotion for the first time. The shot of a tearful Rick dissolves (the classic technique for a flashback in Hollywood cinema from Griffith onwards) via a cross-fade to Paris in 1940. The flashback ends with Rick left at the railway station in the rain. The dissolving effect of the rain creates its own dissolve before a cross-fade back to Rick in his bar over a year later.

The subtle and effective use of flashback and flash forward as more than merely an aid to ease of storytelling, rather as a story in themselves, can be seen in use in *Bad Timing* (Roeg, UK, 1979) and *The End of the Affair* (Jordan, UK, 2000) both edited by Tony Lawson.

Bad Timing begins with Milena (Theresa Russell) being rushed to hospital. The rest of the film is a 'flashback' to the events that led to her overdose. Chronologically this leads us from the leaving of her husband on the Czech–Austrian border through her meeting with Alex (Art Garfunkel), their various ups and downs, her attempted suicide and his 'ravishment' of her. Even within this extended flashback there are many flashbacks. The film ends with the main protagonists meeting by chance several years later – in effect a final flash forward. By that point the terms backwards and forwards have ceased to have much meaning within the films fluid diegesis. The final shot of *Bad Timing* is of a river. This enigmatic ending is certainly a reference to the divisions (East–West, man–woman) that have fuelled the film. It also must surely refer to Heraclitus' famous dictum on the nature of history that one 'cannot enter a river twice in the same place'. Roeg, who has often utilised combinations of flashbacks and flash forwards, often referred to his realisation whilst working in a dubbing studio in the 1940s that editing was a time machine.

The End of the Affair does not flaunt its technique in quite the same overt manner as Roeg's masterpiece. However, in two sequences flashback is used to powerful effect. As the writer Bendricks (played by Ralph Fiennes) climbs his friend's stairs he remembers how he began to make love to Sarah – the man's wife – on those very stairs. The fact that the flashback is *not* visually signalled, indeed is carefully matched, gives it added shock value. A similar technique is used during an aborted rekindling of the affair in a wartime restaurant. Sara leaves, the affair is apparently salvaged by Bendricks chasing and catching her. The viewer only discovers this is a flashback of an earlier assignation when the scene continues with Fiennes still sitting in the restaurant.

The strict linearity of time can also be treated by speeding it up or slowing it down. The slowing down of time has been a stock in trade of film-making since the early experiments in motion photography of Eadweard Muybridge. Speeding up the action has been a stock in trade of comedy films since the Sennet comedies of the 1910s. The use of reiteration of key events, whilst rare, can be seen to good effect in the work of Sergei Eisenstein (see the *Battleship Potemkin* analysis , pp. 48–9), Nic Roeg (e.g. the drowning in *Don't Look Now* (1973)) and Martin Scorsese (e.g. Betsy on the street in *Taxi Driver* (1976)).The retelling of a single event from several points of view has been the narrative form of many films from the classic *Rashomon* (Kurosawa, Japan, 1950) to *Where's the Money, Ronnie?* (Meadows, UK, 1996).

CAUSE AND EFFECT

In the classic narrative events are linked by a cause and effect relationship. This means that we always see and understand the cause of the action taking place. In other words the action is clearly motivated and always focused on the main strands of the narrative. Scenes that do not have a clearly discernible effect are excluded. This leads to a tight structure and an economy of storytelling.

The agents of cause and effect are usually characters, e.g. in *Casablanca* (Curtiz, USA, 1942), Ilsa left Rick in Paris without explanation. This is the primary cause of his cynicism and bitterness and thus motivates many of his actions. Causes may also be natural, e.g. an erupting volcano or typhoon in a disaster movie may be the cause that precipitates the actions of the characters. Once the initial situation is set up, human goals and desires (the different ways that the characters react to the disaster) usually take over.

As spectators we actively seek to link events by means of cause and effect: given an event we tend to imagine either what might have caused it or what it might cause in its turn. This can be seen particularly in detective films where we often start with an effect, e.g. a murdered body, but do not know the cause (motive, method and identity of the murderer). It is the detective's role to satisfy our curiosity and supply the missing causes so that we understand the sequence of events.

CHARACTER

The classic Hollywood narrative is centred around one or two leading characters whose motivations, goals and desires form the body of the narrative. Even in the case of major historical events, e.g. war (or disasters as mentioned above), the focus of the narrative is still on the individual experience of one or two characters and the way in which they react to the situation which becomes the backdrop to or context of their personal experience.

THE HERO

The hero is central to the classic Hollywood narrative in many ways. He is usually male and is likely to be larger than life, i.e. braver, cleverer, more glamorous and exciting than you or me. His importance is signified by his position; he will be in the centre of the frame more than any other character; he will be present in most scenes. He is likely to instigate the action (being in control of the situation) and is usually the agent by which resolution is achieved at the end of the film. Of course there are films with a heroine in the central role, e.g. *Mildred Pierce* (Curtiz, USA, 1945) and many of the films predicated upon the star image of Betty Davis. However, women were more usually cast as the love interest, companion to the hero.

CLOSURE

Closure is the way in which the film ends. It doesn't just stop. All loose ends are tied up, no causes are left dangling and no effects are left unexplained. A new order is established and all the characters are dealt with in some way (usually married or dead). If the film has closure, we are not left to wonder what happened or what is going to happen next, and we should feel that the story has come to an end.

ALTERNATIVE PRACTICE

Most mainstream cinema shares many of the elements of classic narrative cinema but there are powerful alternatives to this mode of storytelling. The Soviet cinema of the 1920s was a heavily politicised mode of representation. In the works of such masters as Eisenstein (*Battleship Potemkin*, 1925 and *October*, 1927), Dovshenko (*Arsenal*, 1929 and *Earth*, 1930) and the FEKS group

(*The New Babylon*, 1929) the presentation and clash of ideas is more important than the 'story' as such. In the documentary work of Dziga Vertov (*The Cine-Eye*, 1924 and *The Man With the Movie Camera*, 1929) an attempt is made to abandon the concept of narrative completely.

Another example of an alternative narrative strategy would be the films of the French New Wave (see Chapter 6). Some of the early films of the group of film-makers that constituted the *Nouvelle Vague*, particularly Jean Luc Godard, abandon the pursuit of verisimilitude in film style (e.g. in the use of jump cuts). Many 'New Wave' films also include sequences that do not appear to be linked by cause and effect and frequently end with ambiguity rather than closure. For example, the narrative of François Truffaut's *The Four Hundred Blows* (France, 1959) is much more fragmentary and episodic than Hollywood (or indeed mainstream French cinema) of the period. Any sense of closure is avoided by leaving the main protagonist reaching the sea only to turn to the camera, his loss at what to do next caught in freeze-frame.

More modern examples of films that deviate from the classic narrative pattern include *Pulp Fiction* (Tarantino, US, 1994), *Sliding Doors* (Howitt, UK/USA, 1998) and *Run Lola Run* (Tykwer, Germany, 1998), although these films all share more elements of the classic narrative than they have dispensed with. *Pulp Fiction* is discussed later in this chapter. *Sliding Doors* presents the viewer with two parallel stories centred around the same central character. Effectively the film is playing with the idea of cause and effect. An initial incident, the getting on a tube train, is presented to us twice. In the first scenario the character gets her train; in the second she misses it. The rest of the film is devoted to showing the consequence and effects of these different initial causes.

By presenting us with two versions of one life happening simultaneously the narrative abandons verisimilitude. This is not real but a magical device, a glimpse into the realm of 'what if?' At the same time once we accept these two co-existing versions of one life, everything about the way in which they are presented to us conforms to the classic narrative pattern. Within each story events are linked by cause and effect, time runs forward and cinematic style is focused on verisimilitude.

Run Lola Run has a similar premise to *Sliding Doors*, this time presenting us with four versions of the same day of Lola's life, one after the other. Small variations at the start of each version of events create a sequence of consequences so that although each story occupies the same time and space and involves the same characters and initial cause, the outcome is different in each case.

THEORY

Narrative can be approached in a formal/theoretical as well as empirical/descriptive manner. Narratology is the formal study of narrative. The Russian formalists, e.g. Viktor Shklovskii, who pioneered this area of study, were writing about literature. Thus, key texts such as *Poetica Kino* 1927 are in fact literary theory used more or less successfully on film. Narratology at its worst can become a dry exercise in defining and differentiating between such arcane terms as *syuzhet* and *fabula*.

The most famous of the narratologists, Vladimir Propp (*The Morphology of the Russian Folk Tale*, first published in 1929), claimed that all narratives share a set of stock characters: Donor, Helper, Princess, Princess's Father, Dispatcher, Hero, False Hero and Villain. These immutable types are engaged in combinations of 31 possible narrative units: 'leaving home', 'prohibition broken', etc. A good deal of transliteration has to take place for this folk-tale-specific material to be brought to bear on individual movies (not based on folk-tales). Thus, rather oddly, Peter Wollen (*Signs and Meaning in the Cinema*, 1972) in an analysis of *North by North West* can claim the double agent is a Princess. At best, Propp can be claimed to have made us think about narrative without simply being carried away by it. However, if we are carried away by a parlour game of spot the (imposed) character type little progress has been made. Rather more fruitful is the work of Bulgarian linguist Tzvetan Todorov.

Todorov developed a basic narrative model of equilibrium, disruption, disequilibrium and equilibrium restored by action. Todorov's model is recommended by its simplicity, by it clearly containing elements of truth about the basic structure of narrative and by his insistence on the fact that the new equilibrium *is* new. Oversimplification could be a criticism levelled at Todorov. None the less, Hollywood script doctors claim there are only seven stories and the 'Holy Grail' is the eighth one.

In the recent past film theory has been greatly influenced by structuralism and its offshoots. Roland Barthes (*Mythologies*, 1957) brought the basic structuralist argument of in-built oppositions to bear on the concept of myth and the functions of popular culture. David Bordwell and his colleagues Staiger and Thompson brought structuralist rigour and an attention to empirical detail to *The Classical Hollywood Cinema: film style and mode of production to 1960* (1985). Bordwell's *Narration in the Fiction Film* (1985) is both an introduction and contribution to this field of study. The book is a subtle, detailed and cinema-specific study of narrative structure. Bordwell's approach leads to a highlighting and analysis of essential elements of cinematic narrative, particularly tense, mood and voice. Bordwell's analysis tends to bring out the complexity of, and interplay between, various elements of the narrative.

It is the authors' contention that developing models of storytelling can really best be seen by a careful deconstruction of the narrative structures of a series of films in chronological order. For our experiment we will take one early, one 'classic' and one contemporary movie: *The Great Train Robbery*, *Stagecoach* and *Pulp Fiction*.

The Great Train Robbery (Porter, 1903) is an example of the basic narrative structure. It is one of the earliest narrative films that succeeds in telling a story that moves between a number of different locations. It was arguably the most popular American film before 1910. It consists of only thirteen shots but these shots provide it with a definite beginning, middle and end although the beginning is fairly abrupt as we plunge straight into the action. There is very little characterisation in the film, which restricts itself to two categories of character: 'goodies' and 'baddies'. These categories are clearly defined by what they *do*. However, due to an inability to delineate representational types, it is not always possible to identify who is who within the frenetic action sequences. Nonetheless, the film ends (before the ground-breaking but rather 'tacked on' close-up) on a moral note with all the 'baddies' dying.

Of greatest interest to the contemporary viewer perhaps is a consideration of the film language, which is not yet sophisticated enough to tell a sophisticated story or delineate character in any depth. Scenes are composed of one shot without the use of close-ups to break the scene down and allow the spectator to focus on character/reaction/detail. The camera remains mostly static with the action unfolding before it. The breaks between scenes are not transitions. They are very abrupt to modern eyes with no attempt at matching in terms of action or physical space. Screen direction is not taken into account, so that on several occasions the bandits run off-screen in one direction and then appear in the next shot running the other way.

What is most apparent from all of this is that whilst a story *is* being told, the film-maker has a limited ability to guide the viewer by highlighting events/details within a scene. In the opening shot the bandits appear in the telegraphic office and hold up the telegraph operator at gunpoint. Through a window towards the right of the screen we see a train pulling up but as the camera remains static the arrival of the train is not highlighted. One of the bandits then crouches down and hides under the telegraph clerk's desk. It is not clear what he is doing until a man appears at the window to the left of the screen. With the bandit's gun trained on him the telegraph clerk sees to this man. The appearance of the train is obviously the cause of the man interrupting the hold-up and both of these events should create suspense. They do not because they are not highlighted in any way but remain details that can easily get lost within the scene which is composed of only one shot. Therefore the narrative has a very episodic nature. One thing happens after another but the connections between them are not always clear. Because the methods of storytelling are limited by the static camera and abrupt editing, aspects of the story get lost.

Another example of this is when the bandits have held up the train and the passengers are disembarking at gunpoint (shot 5). The door of the train from which the passengers are disembarking is centre-frame with a bandit opposite the door pointing his gun at it. The passengers with their hands in the air fill up the screen on both sides. After the last one has got off the train nothing happens. The bandit is still waving his gun at the empty door but there is no action. It is difficult to read this part of the scene; the viewer ends up peering at it to try to work out what is going on. Eventually to the far right of the screen another bandit appears taking valuables from the passengers. The action has obviously continued but off-screen and we have to wait until it catches up with the camera position to see it. At this point a passenger suddenly breaks away from the crowd and gets shot. On a second viewing it is possible to pick him out of the crowd before he makes his move and we can see the actor doing his utmost to indicate what he is going to do. Again this part of the story, though perfectly adequately performed, is lost because there is nothing to guide the viewer.

These comments are not criticisms of Porter. It is to his credit that he created a film that is comprehensible, where the action takes place in different locations (although he doesn't cross-cut to indicate that it is simultaneous) and that was clearly exciting to contemporary audiences. Watching such an early film does help us to understand the range and complexity of devices which have been developed since 1903 through which a film-maker can communicate narrative information.

Stagecoach (Ford, USA, 1939), as well as being the classic Western, the template from which the rest were to follow, is also a perfect example of the classic Hollywood narrative.

- The narrative follows a conventional structure where we clearly see a beginning, middle and end (in that order).
- Events are linked by a cause and effect relationship, which makes motivation clear to the audience; e.g. at the start of the film we have a cause – the murder of Ringo's family – which effects the shoot-out at the end of the film.
- The story is character driven and we understand what drives the characters.
- The role of the hero is important. He instigates much of the action and brings about resolution at the end of the film.
- We see economy of storytelling, where each event serves not only to illuminate character but also to move the story along by triggering the next event. The birth of Lucy's baby is a good example of this. The enforced wait amid the ever-increasing threat of Indian attack is juxtaposed with the images of birth and new life. The humanity (or lack of it) of each of the characters is revealed through their responses to both the increasing danger and the baby. For Dallas and Doc it provides them with redemption, an opportunity to shine. For Gatewood it reveals the true depths of his selfishness. As well as illuminating the characters in this way the scene triggers a further crisis because they can't move Lucy.
- The film has a clear sense of closure where nothing is left dangling or unexplained.
- Apart from the scene of the Indian attack the film follows the rules of continuity editing – the process of piecing the film together so that the joins are invisible, spatial continuity is maintained and the viewer can easily follow the story.

Film theorist André Bazin wrote that: 'Stagecoach is like a wheel, so perfectly made that it remains in equilibrium on its axis in any position.' The structure of the film is certainly very formal. The story takes place over two days and is divided into carefully balanced episodes, e.g. the 12-minute opening scene in Tonto where the characters boarding the stage are carefully and comprehensively introduced is balanced by the arrival in Lordsburg where they disembark and their various goals are quickly resolved.

Much of the richness of the narrative comes from the mixing of such different characters each with their different but clearly defined goals. The characters can in fact be divided into groups. In one we see the apparently respectable people, i.e. Lucy Mallory, Gatewood (actually an embezzler) and Hatfield, whose chivalrous aspiration to protect Lucy marks a return to former values and an abandonment of his selfish gambling. In the second group we have the apparently disreputable characters, i.e. the drunken Doc Boone, Dallas the prostitute and Ringo the outlaw. The progression of the narrative will challenge these appearances; Dallas, Doc and Ringo each find redemption through their humanity. Lucy's snobbery is momentarily lifted only to return when she rejoins society. Hatfield dies having recovered his chivalrous Southern code (his death symbolising the death of the lifestyle and values of the South that he represents). It is Peacock, the solemn whiskey-drummer who presents us with the simplest moral of the film: 'Let us have a little Christian charity toward one another.' Buck and Curly outside the coach act like a chorus on the moral debate within.

These nine disparate characters are held together by two main narrative strands: the perilous journey across a hostile landscape and Ringo's revenge plot; both staple elements of the Western. *Stagecoach* provides us with an example of the classic Hollywood narrative in action. Within this structure there is room for complexity and originality.

Pulp Fiction (Tarantino, 1994) has a more postmodern spin on narrative form. The plot is divided into five distinct parts or episodes. The middle three are signalled by the use of titles:

• Prologue
• Vincent Vega and Marsellus Wallace's Wife
• The Gold Watch
• The Bonnie Situation
• Epilogue

The most notable way in which the film departs from the classic Hollywood narrative is the way in which these five episodes are sequenced. The shuffling of the sequences from within episodes breaks the tradition of the linear narrative, creating a fractured

The narrative fractures, *Pulp Fiction* (1994). Miramax/Buena Vista (courtesy Kobal)

effect where one event does not necessarily follow another. The impact of this comes in the episode of 'The Gold Watch' where we see Butch (Bruce Willis) shoot Vincent (John Travolta). In a traditional linear narrative time would move forward so that we would not see Vincent's character again unless it was clearly marked as a flashback to an earlier time. In the next episode, The 'Bonnie Situation', Vincent reappears. This is not a flashback. The narrative has simply returned to the story of Vincent and Jules.

Pulp Fiction can be read as a parody of the Hollywood 'gangster' film in which Tarantino plays with the characteristics of the genre. In the same way the narrative structure of the film can be seen as a parody of the classic Hollywood narrative structure. It is possible to re-order the events of the film, returning it to the classic Hollywood linear narrative in which the events take place over a period of four days. Why did Tarantino choose to structure the film in this way? It is possible that the structure of the film is a homage to Jean Luc Godard who famously said, 'A film should have a beginning a middle and an end. But not necessarily in that order.' Godard's influence on Tarantino is expressed elsewhere in the film, not least in the name of his production company 'A Band Apart' which is the title of a 1964 Godard film.

Of equal importance to consideration of authorial intention is consideration of the impact the fractured narrative structure has on a viewer. This departure from the traditional mode of representation must disconcert members of an audience raised on the linearity that still dominates mainstream cinema. Although the film might be perceived or categorised as difficult because of its unusual structure it was a huge box-office success, indicating that the ordinary viewer can be entertained by this kind of provocative departure from the norm. To return to the scene described above where Butch kills Vincent, there are a number of very specific effects proceeding from the way the story is organised that highlight the ways in which we respond to the hero/protagonist of a story. Both Butch and Vincent are murderers and yet when they occupy centre stage of their respective stories we identify with their different conflicts dilemmas and desires.

In the preceding episode, 'Vincent Vega and Marsellus Wallace's Wife', we have just seen Vincent struggle to overcome the catastrophe of Mia's overdose. It is a shock to find him relegated to the role of bit-part villain in Butch's story. By the time Butch picks up Vincent's gun we are firmly engaged with Butch and the desire to see him escape. Until the identity of his opponent is revealed we want Butch to succeed: to be the killer/hero, not the victim. These feelings are called into question when Tarantino reveals Butch's opponent to be Vincent. Our identification with the hero is no longer a straightforward identification with Butch, because we also perceive Vincent as a hero. We also want him to succeed/win. Vincent's death therefore has an impact and shock value that is the direct result of the way the narrative is structured. The death fits comfortably with Butch's narrative but is a very uncomfortable conclusion to Vincent's narrative because it is perfunctory and he is no longer centre stage, no longer important. The reappearance of Vincent mitigates against these feelings creating a kind of fairy-tale element. We know that he dies, but he's back, so does it matter?

SOUND

Up to this point in order to concentrate on visual elements of storytelling we have ignored the role of sound. However, from the very earliest days of cinema, sound has been one of the key devices by which a film-maker can counteract the fragmentary nature of film to tell, propel, or enhance its storytelling properties.

Edits may be frequent, constantly presenting us with changing visual images, but sound is likely to be more continuous, carrying over from one shot to the next and so helping to connect the images and provide continuity from one shot to the next. Sound also provides the viewer with sound motifs which contribute to their engagement with the narrative and aid a sense of completeness. The extra dimension that sound adds to a film has been acknowledged since the early days of cinema. Live music, often just a piano but on occasions a full orchestra (in the case of *The Birth of a Nation* (Griffith, USA, 1913), was supplied to aid the storytelling and mood of the pictures. Adding sound to film as part of the production process took several decades. This is less a function of the difficulty of doing so than how economically successful silent film was for so long. In 1927 the Warner Brothers took the plunge into sound production with *The Jazz Singer*.

The use of musical soundtracks, though common to most films, is paradoxical in that it does not fit into the realist tradition (see Chapter 1) whereby verisimilitude (the appearance of reality) is of prime importance. It is not realistic to have orchestral music appearing apparently from nowhere, music to which the characters themselves seem perfectly oblivious . Yet it is perfectly usual. A scene where the most painstaking attempts have been made to create the illusion of reality can be overlaid with the best efforts of a full (though invisible) orchestra and we accept it, not as a distraction, but as part of the film. It is one of the areas where we willingly suspend our disbelief and get on with enjoying the spectacle of drama, of which that music is a part.

Music is a very powerful means of suggesting mood, creating drama and suspense, hinting that something terrible/significant/climactic is going to happen. Music can be used to indicate that a character's feelings and characters can, and often do, have their own theme tunes which recur throughout a film. Music then, can support and develop the meanings suggested by the *mise en scène*, cinematography and editing. It can draw our attention to certain scenes, highlight features of the narrative and hint at what is to come. (How often have you watched a horror or a thriller and experienced the creeping sense of dread signalled by the music that something terrible is going to happen?)

We do more than accept and react to the presence of music. We read it. Our ability to 'read' the connections between non-diegetic music and diegetic visuals allows film-makers to utilise sound as a form of illustration. Throughout his career Martin Scorsese has used popular songs in particularly engaging and exiting ways. Scorsese's films are packed with a host of thrilling sound/action juxtapositions. In the opening sequence of *Mean Streets* (1973), where Charlie's head hits the pillow in time to the opening drum beat of the Ronettes 'Be My Baby', the pivotal sequence in *Casino*

(1995) as Ginger catches the eye of Sam to the soundtrack of 'Slippin' and Slidin' ' (Little Richard), snares him to 'Love is Strange' (Mickey and Sylvia) and seduces him to 'Heart of Stone' (The Rolling Stones). In *Bringing out the Dead* (1999) Frank has a most disturbing drug experience to the accompaniment of 'Rang Tang Ding Dong' by the Cellos. In recent years Scorsese's position as the most original exploiter of popular music has been challenged by both Spike Lee and Quentin Tarantino.

Music is obviously not the only source of sound and, as with the other areas of film language, we can divide sound up into different categories. The simplest way of doing this is to divide sound into two categories:

- diegetic sound
- non-diegetic sound.

Diegetic means belonging to the world of the film, so diegetic sound incorporates all those sounds that are motivated by the film world. Diegetic sound can be 'on-screen' or 'off-screen'. 'On-screen sound' simply proceeds from the images we can see. 'Off-screen sound is still diegetic but we are left to imagine rather than see the source of the sound, e.g. we may see the interior of a flat and hear the doorbell ring. We don't need to see the door or the doorbell but can infer their presence from the off-screen sound. Off-screen sound is particularly effective in creating suspense and fear of something we can hear but can't see, e.g. *The Blair Witch Project* (Sanchez and Myrick, USA, 1999), *Jurassic Park* (Spielberg, USA, 1993).

Diegetic sound would include:

- dialogue and all other sounds made by the actors, e.g. laughing, screaming (but not voice-over narration – see non-diegetic sound). The things people say is not only a way of drawing character but also of stimulating an audience's response to that character. Dialogue is a very clear and direct way of introducing information which helps to explain actions and motivations. Characters can also easily fill in explanations of events and indeed describe events or parts of events not actually seen. Sadly, this ease too often leads to dialogue (or more often monologue) replacing film storytelling of any subtlety;
- sound effects suggested by the setting e.g. phones and doorbells ringing, television and radio in the background, traffic noises, footsteps, dogs barking, etc;

- music, if we can see that it is sourced in the world of the film; for example the characters attend an opera (*Pretty Woman* (Marshall, USA, 1990), *The Godfather Part III*) or put on a record or dance, e.g. *Strictly Ballroom* (Luhrmann, Australia, 1992) and *Saturday Night Fever* (Badham, 1977).

Non-diegetic sound does not belong to the world of the film, so this would include:

- The musical score or soundtrack (the invisible orchestra discussed above) – although in *Eyes Wide Shut* (Kubrick, UK, 1999) the director plays a trick by beginning with an ostensibly non-diegetic theme which then stops when a character turns off a diegetic sound system.
- Voice-over narration – a technique whereby the voice of one of the characters accompanies the images telling us the story. For the best example of this see the films of Martin Scorsese – *Taxi Driver* (1976), *The Age of Innocence* (1993).

In the case of non-diegetic sound we can have

- parallel sound
- contrapuntal sound.

Effective use of both parallel and contrapuntal sound can be seen in *Jaws* (Spielberg, 1973). The 'parallel sound' of laughter complements images of children playing on the beach. The impact of 'contrapuntal sound' can be felt when the Jaws theme enters the soundtrack as the children continue playing near the water's edge.

SOUND IN ACTION: *RAIDERS OF THE LOST ARK*

In Chapter 1 we discussed how meaning was created by the *mise en scène* in the opening sequence of *Raiders of the Lost Ark*. Now we would like to return to the same sequence and consider how many of the effects are created and underlined through the use of sound.

The initial images present us with a mysterious figure and his followers traversing a jungle terrain inhabited by unknown dangers.

Suspense (about what might be lurking around the next corner) and a sense of mystery are central to this scene and are created largely through the non-diegetic music. We hear deep ominous notes from a variety of instruments, including flute, drums, woodwind and strings. These are constructed into a slow haunting melody that reflects the measured progress of the travellers.

Whilst the non-diegetic sound creates mood, the diegetic sound functions slightly differently to enhance the sense of verisimilitude. The different settings in the sequence, exterior in the jungle and interior in the temple are given a sense of authenticity by the sound effects. In the jungle we hear the chatter of birds and monkeys, the clink of the mule's harness, the chopping sound of a machete cutting its way through the undergrowth. In the temple we hear the crunch of footsteps on stone.

The first climactic moment comes with the discovery of a demonic stone carving, evidence of the existence of the temple. The sense that this is a dramatic moment in the narrative is created almost solely through the use of sound. The music punctuates the action, crescendoing suddenly to signify a moment of drama. This happens in conjunction with the diegetic sound, the frantic beating of birds' wings creating the sense of surprise; the scream of the native who makes the discovery creating fear. This sets the pattern for the rest of the film. Moments of drama and significance are highlighted by changes in the music which arrest the viewer's attention and signal that something important is taking place. Music is also used to echo or reflect the images, for example the pizzicato strings reflecting the scurrying movement of the tarantula spiders in the temple, the rousing theme tune that speaks of daring and adventure first heard when 'Indy' escapes in the plane at the end of this first sequence.

It is an indication of the skill of the film-makers that so much of the narrative is communicated through pictures and sound other than dialogue, but of course dialogue is important too. In this sequence we see it used to relate the bare minimum of information. Its role is to increase the sense of drama already created by other means rather than bearing responsibility for creating such drama. Before they enter the temple Indy's sidekick (played by Alfred Molina) informs us that 'no-one has come out of there alive'. We already know that this will not deter the hero.

Spielberg and his company of film-makers are both skilled proponents and a product of a seemingly all-pervasive entertainment machine we know as Hollywood – the subject of the next chapter.

Some things to watch out for and consider

Film narrative can be approached in a number of different ways but we are suggesting two areas of analysis that may prove fruitful.

1. To what extent does the narrative of the film in question conform to or depart from the classic Hollywood narrative?
2. How is narrative information communicated?
    - Through images: consider the specific choices being made in the *mise en scène*, cinematography and editing any of which may be used to highlight a detail, illustrate a character or move the story along.
    - Through sound, which we can break down as follows.

Diegetic sound
- What different types of diegetic sound can you identify, e.g. dialogue, sound effects, on-screen and off-screen sound.
- What is the function and effect of these different types of sound?

Non-diegetic sound
- What different types of non-diegetic sound can you identify? What is the function and effect of the non-diegetic sound within the film/scene?

Is the sound parallel or contrapuntal?
How does the sound work in conjunction with the editing?

5 Classical Hollywood (as form and as institution)

You ain't seen nothing yet.
(Al Jolson in *The Jazz Singer* (1928))

This chapter is an analytical history of the Hollywood 'dream factory', the nature of and reasons for the development of its institutional mode of representation. This history should be viewed as a (very successful) struggle to expand and consolidate a national and international market and to develop niches within the market. The individual studio styles (e.g. Paramount's gloss, Warner Brothers' 'realism' and MGM's glamour) can be seen as variations on a theme of efficient craftsmanship of a supremely high quality. The power and effectiveness of this culmination of craft will be illustrated by institutional readings of *Casablanca* (Curtiz, 1942) and *Gone With the Wind* (Fleming, 1939). The final section of this chapter seeks to explain how 'Hollywood' adapted and survived the legal and socio-economic travails of the 1940s and 1950s and flourished as 'New Hollywood'.

Let us not forget that cinema is an industrial process and no more so than in the USA. Successful film-making is reliant on somebody (but not always the *same* body) having a firm understanding of the processes of finance, organisation, production, distribution, marketing and exhibition. 'Hollywood' during the first half of the twentieth century developed a system by which individual institutional bodies (the studios) could and did perform all of these functions in a finely tuned industrial manner.

As part of this industrial process the 'dream factories' developed a way of telling stories – and presenting those stories visually – that was ubiquitous and institutionalised. Thus the terms 'classic Hollywood film' (CHF) and the 'institutional mode of representation' (IMR) have become synonyms.

In its early years, world cinema was dominated by French and British companies. The French had the natural advantage of being the first producers of film. However, the Lumière Brothers were pioneers rather than astute entrepreneurs and Georges Méliès died penniless. Charles Pathé moved from selling photographs to making and (crucially) distributing films in 1901. Along with Gaumont – another photographic company – Pathé presided over the expansion of the industry via vertical integration, i.e. ownership of production, distribution and exhibition.

By 1908 Pathé sold twice as many films in the USA than all of the American production companies put together. Pathé built a film-processing factory in New York and opened a studio in New Jersey. The British had also seized upon the commercial possibilities of moving pictures. Robert Paul had not only developed his own camera equipment, unlike the Lumières he was willing to sell it. Cecil Hepworth and James Williamson, amongst others, were making and selling short films to travelling salesmen and music hall exhibitors in the early years of the twentieth century. In 1907 the first purpose-built cinemas opened and what followed was an exponential growth in exhibition. In 1908 there were three companies dealing in permanent cinema exhibition. By 1910 the number was over 1500. The number of cinemas in Britain doubled from 3500 in 1910 to over 7000 by 1915.

British film companies increasingly concentrated on the immediately lucrative distribution sector. Foreign product was cheaper because much of the production cost had already been recouped at home. By 1915 only 15 per cent of films released in Britain were British made. The profits made from these films went to distributors who used it to buy more foreign product. This trend coincided with an enormously effective US export drive beginning in 1908–9.

In 1913 Pathé, along with the other French 'majors', cut back on its own production to concentrate on its vast distribution network. By 1917 50 per cent of the French market was supplied by US product. In a deeply symbolic move Pathé even sold off their film stock production capacity to an American company, Eastman Kodak.

The momentum for the phenomenal growth and increasing

domestic and global power of the US film industry had already begun before the First World War. In 1900 the USA was the largest market for film in the world with more cinemas per capita than any other state. The early days of American cinema – after Edison exhibited his Vitascope in April 1896 – were typified by commercial anarchy. More and more 'companies' engaged in nefarious copying activities. Films and projection became poorer and poorer in quality. The industry was saved by current affairs (audience demand for pictures of the Spanish–American War), religion (demand for moving pictures to accompany 'passion plays' aimed at the influx of non-English speaking, southern European immigrants) and sport (demand for coverage of boxing matches as several states banned the sport itself).

American Mutoscope became the first US 'major' by producing good-quality 70 mm prints and added 'biograph' to their name. Edison tried equipment copyright litigation but lost. This was the signal for more legitimate companies to become involved in the movie business. Edison, having split from Vitagraph, began his own company in order to make longer films. The move was towards quality – particularly in the work of Edwin S. Porter – and efficiency – including the use of a glass-roofed studio to maximise filming time. Porter was responsible not for the invention of narrative film (as he was wont to claim) but of refining storytelling to new heights, including the use of cross-cutting and close-ups, with films such as *The Great Train Robbery* (1903).

The US industry focused on stabilisation. Part of this stabilisation process was to capitalise on the increased leisure time of industrial workers by building permanent movie theatres in the major conurbations. These new cheap but comfortable halls became known as 'nickelodeons' (a nickel, or 5 cents, was charged for admission). Admission prices were kept low because of the growth of a distribution system which meant exhibitors could rent rather than buy films. Renting also meant that programmes could be changed regularly – in some centres twice weekly.

The 'nickelodeons' launched the movie industry careers of a number of entrepreneurs, including the Warner Brothers, Louis B. Mayer, William Fox, Carl Laemmle (who founded Universal) and Adolph Zukor (Paramount). These men – who built the Hollywood system – thus began their careers in the movies by learning what the audience wanted.

Although less hampered by illegal copying, the industry was still hamstrung by litigation. Edison had come to terms on patents with American Mutoscope and Biograph. Thus the big players worked together through the Motion Picture Patents Company (MPPC) which acted as a magnet for others, including Vitagraph. Foreign companies were blocked from joining the club. The MPPC controlled domestic production by licensing equipment and – after signing a mutual monopoly deal with Eastman-Kodak – supply of film stock. Thus the whole industry was mutually self-regulated. However, this system was dubious legally. In 1909 Laemmle – who had become the US's biggest distributor – split from the MPPC to form the Independent Motion Picture Corporation. Most of the major distributors did likewise. In 1912 the MPPC sued Laemmle for using 'their' projection equipment. Over the next decade the industry abandoned internecine warfare and organised itself into a system of competitive co-operation exemplified by the activities of the Motion Picture Producers and Distributors of America. The MPPDA began – and has continued through various name changes – as a structure for organising companies which are essentially competitors around an under-standing of mutual benefits. The organisation began as a response to the threat of censorship. Faced with the possibility of external – i.e. non-commercial – interference, the companies chose self-censorship.

The MPPDA began as a mechanism for self-censorship under the auspices of Will Hays. Hays was a former postmaster general and a publicity agent for the Republican Party. Very soon the companies involved realised the potential of the association as a conduit for information exchange and as a pressure group on government policy. The Foreign Department became a powerful weapon in the campaign against European defensive trade restrictions. In 1926 Hays lobbied Congress to form the Motion Pictures Division of the Department of Commerce, thus institutionalising the US Government's support of their film industry, by then known simply as 'Hollywood'.

A key element in the consolidation of the American film industry was the move west to Hollywood. In the first decade of the twentieth century the industry was based in New York, New Jersey and Chicago. The film companies were businesses and American business was based on the East Coast. However, the light was not consistently good even on a day-to-day basis. Poor light led to delays and delays cost money. Some of the New York companies tried filming in Florida. The Chicago firms began winter filming on the West Coast. In 1908 the Selig Company filmed outside Los Angeles. In 1909 they built a studio. The New York based Ince Company did the same. By 1910 Biograph were sending their top director – D. W. Griffith – for the winter. He was just too expensive a commodity to be left to be resting for extended periods.

Los Angeles had clean air, was dry and benefited from predictable weather. Real estate was cheap (at least in 1910) and the area was located near a pleasant coast line. The countryside was also well suited for filming Westerns – fast becoming the most popular genre with American audiences.

The US industry emerged from World War I as an efficient production, distribution and exhibition machine. The leadership of the industry had the good sense to consolidate and strengthen their hegemonic position in the following years. It is worth iterating that the US industry has the in-built natural advantage of the biggest domestic market. At the end of the war it was also able to exploit the comparative advantage over Europe of not having to reconstruct its infrastructure and the absolute advantage of an economic boom. Surplus capital was looking for investment opportunities. None were more glamorous than the movies. The money that flooded into the film companies was used to fuel unprecedented vertical integration.

Paramount, the distribution wing of Famous Players-Lasky, began buying movie theatres in 1920. In 1922 they merged with Bela Ban and Katz, a Chicago firm which dominated exhibition in the Midwest. The merger created the first truly national production–exhibition–distribution company: Paramount-Publix. Marcus Loew, who began as a nickelodeon manager, bought the production company Metro (owned by Louis B. Mayer) in 1919. In 1924 they bought Goldwyn Pictures to create MGM. The other 'major' was First National created by a group of East Coast exhibitors after World War I.

MGM and Publix never owned the majority of the USA's 15 000 movie theatres but they did own the luxurious 'first run' cinemas in the big cities. Their products gained the national press and radio attention. These giants also developed a way of maximising profits from the theatres they did not own via 'block bookings'. If an independent exhibitor wished to show the high-profile studio films (backed by high-profile publicity) they would have to buy a whole package of studio product. It was not unknown for small exhibitors to have to hire a whole year's programming in one 'block'. The good news for American cinema was that the 'majors' were owned and run by people who had a vested interest in rein-vesting the huge profits in more films. Along with the 'big three' initial 'majors' stood the 'little five' – defined by less exhibition capacity – Universal, Fox, the Producers' Distribution Corporation, the Film Booking Office (which formed the basis of RKO) and Warner Brothers (who joined the big league by invest-ing the huge profits from 'Rin Tin Tin' movies into the develop-ment of sound).

These studios became huge industrial enterprises. The studio heads were faced with rocketing overheads. As the movie indus-try became bigger and bigger, more and more people, from prop-erty developers to organised labour, required more and more payment. The development of a star system, which made sound commercial sense (see Chapter 8), was in itself costly. Zukor's move to take over Paramount was followed by a merger with Famous Players. Suddenly he had to find the cash to pay a whole stable of stars, including Gloria Swanson, Mary Pickford and Douglas Fairbanks as well as big name directors like Griffith, Sennett and DeMille. Zukor was uniquely blessed but not uniquely pressured to make more money, more quickly. All of the Studio Heads needed to produce more and more films. They wanted to do so more and more efficiently. The challenge was to develop an industrial product. The answer was a division of labour within a film factory. The producer (a studio employee) would be responsible for the co-ordination of individual products. The director (also contracted to the studio) would oversee the actual filming. A crew of studio-contracted technicians would make the film along with actors, also under contract. All these employees would move from one production to the next. In the scenario department separate writers or teams of writers worked on plotting, dialogue, and so on.

In order to co-ordinate all of this activity the studios required a 'continuity script'. In essence this was the template for the film. It allowed everyone to know where they were. The producer could work on costs, the designers knew in advance what was required and, after shooting, the editor would have a list of scenes (to match with the numbers on the slates before each shot). Regularisation became a goal in itself. Plots became standardised. Film projects were produced according to the rules of particular genres and sold as such. Matching – in effect only a matter of across the board co-ordination – became the imperative.

The term 'institutional mode of representation' carries with it a host of ideological, political, sociological and economic reasons and results. In film-making terms the IMR (and thus the 'classic' Hollywood film) is characterised by its craft of smoothness. This smoothness is the result of two main elements:

- conventional narrative structure
- continuity editing.

The conventional (or institutionalised) narrative structure is – at its simplest – beginning, middle, end. The film will begin with an equilibrium. The narrative is triggered or set in motion by a disruption which develops to a new equilibrium (resolution). In the institutional mode of representation/classic Hollywood film everything is tied up neatly by the end. Thus the audience is given a satisfying sense of closure. In the conventional narrative, events are connected by cause and effect. The story is easy to follow and understand. This requires a number of film-making techniques centred around the idea of continuity editing. A 'classic' example of this (as discussed in Chapter 3) is *To Have and Have Not*.

The narrative drive of the CHF is how the problem/disruption is resolved. This resolution is usually performed by the hero. The audience will have been given ample opportunity to bond and identify with this individual and most clearly delineated and motivated character by narrative and cinematic devices. Within the narrative the hero will occupy screen space more than any other character. In addition the hero will dominate the screen space when on camera. Cinematic identification will be developed by the 'eye-line match'. It is a tribute to the economy of the IMR that a method of making screen space coherent can also be used as means of identification. Thus, at key moments the audience sees the world through the eyes of the heroic protagonist.

Hollywood film does not present its audience with 'reality'. However, it does have a powerful appearance of reality (verisimilitude). This begins with *mise en scène* and continues through cinematography. Action and space is always presented as to make it understandable. Thus a sequence will start with an 'establishing shot' and obey the 180-degree rule and the 30-degree rule (maximum and minimum camera movement between shots) to avoid a disruptive 'jump cut'. Cuts need matching and changes of scene need a variation in matching. The eye-line match: a shot of a look, followed by a shot of the object being looked at (along with believable characters) leads to spectator engagement. The audience likes it. They buy tickets. The studio system – founded by commercial exhibitors – never forgot that cinema was a business enterprise. The system saw an exponential rise in the cinema audience and produced a vast amount of product tailor-made to attract paying customers. *Casablanca* and *Gone with the Wind* can serve as examples of how that product worked.

Michael Curtiz's (or perhaps more accurately Warner Bros') *Casablanca* began as a product of the Hollywood Studio system. The film was made in 'typical' circumstances, quickly and economically. At under 1 million dollars the production cost was typical of Warner's relatively frugal budget for an A-grade movie. The script was frequently being re-written as shooting continued. Only very late in the shooting of the film did star Ingrid Bergman discover how it was going to end (legend says on the very last day of shooting). Bogart's famous last line, 'I think this is the beginning of a beautiful friendship', was dubbed in one month after shooting had finished. Claude Rains' memorable – and oft-quoted – 'round up the usual suspects' was another last-minute addition to the film.

The film itself is 'typical' in its plot structure and presentation. A mysterious man (Rick) runs a bar in Casablanca. He is clearly world weary. A beautiful woman arrives in the city. Any information about their relationship that would be too tedious to relay in dialogue is presented in flashback. Various interesting characters pass through the bar in order either to push the story on or add some variety to the diegesis. The audience's interest is held by the 'will she (Elsa) won't she' intrigue. The final twist is that Elsa does *not* stay with glamorous Rick but leaves with heroic Victor. The final anti-Nazi pay-off is a sweetening of the pill.

The *mise en scène*, cinematography and editing style is absolutely in keeping with the smooth and easily understood allure of the IMR. The film is a beautifully crafted piece of product; it is also very entertaining and very memorable. A number of elements combine to make *Casablanca* so unforgettable among the thousands of mass-produced studio films. The clarity of structure endemic to the institutional mode allows the writers (Epstein, Epstein and Koch) the space to insert crackling dialogue and a series of exchanges or *bons mots* that have entered cinema history. Some of the dialogue from the film has penetrated popular culture to such an extent that lines are wantonly misquoted ('Play it again, Sam') and a phrase, much used as an epithet, can serve as the title to another movie (*The Usual Suspects*; Singer, USA, 1995).

The overwhelming appeal of the film to mass audiences over several decades resides in the sense of glamour which pervades the film. To some extent this glamour is a result of *mise en scène* and cinematography. Central to the films appeal is the numinous quality of stardom exhibited by both Bogart and Bergman (and the chemistry between the two). The concept of stardom – so central to the appeal of mainstream cinema – is further explored in Chapter 8.

It is important to note that the institutional mode of representation's ability to produce truly memorable and outstanding work mitigates any thoughtless attempt to see it as in any way 'easy' or – even worse – 'careless'. The classic Hollywood film as a model of production and as a storytelling medium was so strong that it was available for adaptation and development without losing its strengths. An example of the power of the IMR was its ability to survive expansion into the realms of fabled epic, e.g. *Gone with the Wind* (Fleming, 1939).

Gone With The Wind was meant from the start to be an epic: big, broad, expensive and long. It won nine Oscars. It is generally held to be the most popular American historical film ever made. It is still in the list of the top 20 money-making films of all times and would probably come in first today if inflation were taken into account. It opened in the second week of December 1939, and by New Year's Day had sold a million dollars worth of tickets. In London, it opened in 1940 and played for a record 232 consecutive weeks. Its 1976 American TV première was the highest rated single

The end of an era, *Gone with the Wind* (1939). Selznick/MGM (courtesy Kobal)

network programme ever broadcast. The *Gone With The Wind* story has been transported to myth.

Gone with the Wind was adapted from a novel by Margaret Mitchell, an Atlanta newspaper reporter, which she based on stories of the old South which she heard as a child. The story was published in 1936 and broke sales records as a book.

The film was produced by David O. Selznick in conjunction with MGM. He negotiated a lot of control. He saw the novel's huge potential as a top box-office film. War and the heroic Rhett Butler for the men; romance and the emotional Scarlett O'Hara for the women. It was both a 'man's movie' and a 'women's picture' at the same time.

Once Selznick had bought up the rights to the book, he had to set about casting the picture. Gable was an obvious choice for Rhett, but Selznick gained a publicity coup basically by publicly auditioning America for an actress to play the part: the search for Scarlett. Fourteen hundred candidates were allegedly screen tested. Selznick really spun the drama out: on 10 December, 1938, Selznick shot the famous burning of Atlanta sequence with stunt doubles standing in for Gable and the still uncast Scarlett O'Hara. According to the legend, in the light of the flames of the Atlanta set, Selznick's brother, an agent, introduced him to his new client, Vivien Leigh. Leigh was cast on the spot.

Selznick was not the director. None the less, he took a hands-on approach to the development, creation and packaging of the product. He controlled the film before, during and after assigning a director and cast. Selznick fired the first director – George Cukor – on the pleadings of Clark Gable (who thought Cukor was a 'woman's director'). Victor Fleming replaced Cukor. During shooting Selznick oversaw every shot. He saw the rushes before the crew.

The production proceeded on an epically expensive scale: 59 leading and supporting players, 2400 extras, 90 sets, women's costumes alone cost $100,000 to buy and another $10,000 to launder. The film's producer had pretensions to be authentic to historical detail. A hoard of advisers were bought in: a Southern dialogue coach, an expert on Southern etiquette and a historical architect specialising in the American Civil War. Production costs topped 3.5 million dollars (close to $300 million in today's money), with another half a million spent on a very large number of prints, publicity and advertising.

In the post-war period this kind of Babylonian excess was under threat. The threat came from two directions: a new medium, i.e. TV, and the American constitution.

In 1946 the US film industry celebrated its best box-office year ever. Export markets closed by the Second World War began to open up again and those markets were starting on their post-war recovery. However, the hegemony of the big studios was under attack by the Supreme Court. In 1938 the US Government had finally attempted to pursue anti-trust proceedings against Paramount Pictures. In 1948 the Supreme Court finally decided against Paramount. The 'Big Five' (Paramount, Warners, MGM, Fox and RKO) and 'Little Three' (Universal, Columbia and United Artists) were forced to sell their stake in the exhibition sector and abandon the policy of block booking.

Demographic changes in the USA had a profound effect on film-viewing patterns. The audience continued its move away from city centres which had begun before the war. The increased availability of cheap automobiles – and low cost fuel – accelerated this trend. The post-war 'baby boom' also tended to keep people at home. They turned to the radio and increasingly to television for their entertainment. By 1960 90 per cent of American homes had a TV set.

The initial reaction of the US majors to the 'threat' of TV was to refuse to work with the new medium. However, as early as 1949 Columbia realised that TV was simply a new medium for distributing its product. The other majors quickly abandoned attempts to attack Columbia and joined the feast. TV created a huge demand for back catalogue, which was costing money to store with, up until then, no income potential. The industry did not abandon its theatrical options. Realising that the audience now had many options for its entertainment dollar, the major companies focused on film-going as an event. Mainstream US films got bigger and bigger and the theatrical experience became a more comfortable experience involving catering and access to other leisure activities.

The loosening of the majors' grip on film production was an opportunity for the growth of independent producers. These (initially) small companies operated on a film at a time basis, attracting finance through packaging their productions to financiers, including but not exclusively the studios. The big prize was to get a distribution deal with a major. This ultimate goal was entirely attainable because the majors saw independent production as the key to cutting their own overheads. By the mid-1960s almost all US film production was 'independent'. For the studios production meant – if anything – television programmes.

The 'Little Three' (Universal, Columbia and United Artists) actually got more access to theatres due to the Paramount decision and the end of block booking. Their product was often more adventurous in its subject matter and presentation, and thus invigorated the mainstream. Outstanding examples include Columbia's *On the Waterfront* (1954), United Artists' *The Sweet Smell of Success* (1957) and Universal's *Touch of Evil* (1959).

The independent companies ranged from Hitchcock or Kubrick working through Universal's facilities to no-budget operations like Sam Arkoff's AIP. AIP was home to a shoestring production outfit headed by Roger Corman. Corman boasted that he could make a film in less than a week for less than $100,000 (when Hollywood movies were often budgeted at 1 million plus). Corman directed a series of inventive horror movies including *The Fall of the House of Usher* (1960) and *The Masque of the Red Death* (1963). As a producer of cheap 'exploitation' movies Corman has been responsible for launching the careers of many of the great figures of American cinema; Scorsese and De Niro included.

It is a signal of the adaptive strength of Hollywood that the major studios have co-opted the talent unearthed by Corman and his like to enrich the mainstream. Examples of Hollywood's ability to co-opt foreign talent is nothing new. US producers have spotted and poached talent from Chaplin to Lang to Hitchcock and beyond. This ability has continued in the post-war years, particularly in the use of European cinematographers (e.g. Kovacs, Storaro) and the more or less successful hiring of European and Asian auteurs (e.g. Roman Polanski, Wim Wenders, Luc Besson and John Woo).

Mainstream American cinema was fast to learn from 'art' cinema – particularly the French 'New Wave' and the 'New York School' around John Cassavetes. Hollywood has even been successful in co-opting the values and iconography of the counter-cultures or subcultures from *Easy Rider* (Fonda, USA, 1969) to *Pulp Fiction* (Tarantino, USA, 1994).

It is absolutely apposite that the 'New Hollywood' chapter of Thompson and Bordwell's *Film History* (1995) should be subtitled 'Hollywood Continued'. The US film industry has never ceased to be a very sophisticated business operation. The big studios were not dinosaurs; they adapted to the changes in the environment whilst strengthening their competitive advantages.

The US film industry – Hollywood for short – remains a powerful, well-organised exporting machine because of its ability to utilise every breakthrough in the audio-visual media, whether that be product or delivery via new media, etc., linked to an understanding of the global market. Ian Jarvie in *Hollywood's Overseas Campaign: The North Atlantic Movie Trade 1920–1950* (1992) points to: 'The coherent orchestration of the component parts of the industry through the Motion Picture Producers and Distributors of America.'

Even in the 1950s it was clear that the Paramount decision had not completely emasculated the major companies. The independents needed access to transcontinental distribution. In the period of the Reagan Administration (1981–88) and since, the majors have regained some of their control over all sectors of the industry. Their control over exhibition abroad has never been seriously threatened by government intervention. In addition the 'majors' – via the MPPA – continued to set the agenda on trade. The central role of the MPPA in American affairs was symbolically confirmed when suggestions that, as long-term head Joe Venuti came close to retirement, its next head should be Bill Clinton.

This institutional analysis should not blind us to the powerful attractiveness of its product. Hollywood's product has been tested in a very competitive market-place and backed by a sense of confidence that it is – if not the best – certainly the most entertaining product available. None the less there are other ways to make films – as will be explored in the next chapter.

6 The film industry outside of the Hollywood institutional mode

My eyes still hurt from reading that movie.
(Scott Roper comments on European film (*Metro*, 1993))

This chapter consists of individual readings of 'institutional modes of representation' which could be – indeed were – seen as alternatives to the 'classic Hollywood film'.

* Soviet cinema, 1918–48
* Italian neo-realism
* the French New Wave
* Dogme '95

SOVIET CINEMA, 1918–1948

The first quarter century of Soviet cinema was roughly contemporaneous with Hollywood's golden age. Like Hollywood, the Soviet film industry was also busy creating a national myth and trying to dominate an international market-place.

The first showing of moving pictures in the Russian Empire took place on 4 May 1896 – a Lumière Brothers show just five months after the Paris première. The Lumière company and its rival Pathé both saw Russia as a lucrative market – showing their films at fairground side-shows. Russian fiction film began with

Drankov's *Stenka Razin*, released 15 October 1908. The film version
of a Russian legend was played as a historical melodrama focus-
ing on bucolic behaviour and singing the popular song 'Down the
Mother Volga'. Within two months Alexander Khanzhonkov –
Drankov's great domestic rival – presented his *Drama in a Gypsy
Camp Near Moscow*.

When the film-makers of pre-Revolutionary Russia turned to
urban subjects they presented their cities as a sight of opulence
and ruination. This becomes the 'Russian style' – rather naughty,
very polished, very mannered. Stylistically the films were not *that*
different from American films of the time, except for a tendency
towards longer shot-length and sad endings. The top director was
Yakov Protazanov. The big stars were Ivan Mozhukin and Vera
Kholodnaia. They were very theatrical in their approach to screen
acting.

The great master of early Russian cinema was Evgeni Bauer. In
1914 Khanzhonkov presented Bauer's *Child of the Big City*. The film
– a story of innocence corrupted – ends with the ruined young
man lying dead on the steps of his ex-mistress' house. In 1917, as
the Russian Empire collapsed, Bauer made *The Alarm* with a
young art director named Lev Kuleshov, an art student who gave
it up to make pictures. For a brief moment the cinema of tsarist
Russia and the future Soviet cinema crossed paths.

In February 1917 – after popular uprisings in Russian cities – the
Tsar abdicated. In October 1917 the rather ineffective 'Provisional
Government' was removed from office in a coup by the
Bolsheviks. Once in power the Bolsheviks were determined to
utilise the power of cinema. As their leader Lenin put it: 'For us the
most important of all the arts is cinema.'

The problem for Lenin and his party was that 'the cinema' had
gone missing. The capitalists did not like Lenin, so they left,
often burying films and equipment first. The Bolsheviks did not
give up. They nationalised the (non-existent) film industry in
February 1918 and set up a special cinema section in the
Commissariat of the Enlightenment. Krupskaia – Lenin's wife –
took charge.

Life was hard. The new state was crippled by a civil war. None
the less, youth flocked to the film industry. The kindergarten of the
new Soviet Cinema was war newsreel. Many of the early masters,
e.g. Eisenstein's cinematographer Tisse and documentary auteur
Dziga Vertov, learnt their trade there. Lev Kuleshov returned from
newsreel duty in the civil war as a veteran of war and cinema

(aged 20). He ran his own workshop at the State Film School (GIK), largely because he was the only experienced film-maker left in the Soviet Union. He developed acting technique by staging 'films without film'. Making a virtue of the famine in film stock he launched a series of experiments which led to the development of montage (see Chapter 3) and the militant belief that the essence of cinema was in its editing. Montage is editing – but editing that emphasises dynamic, sometimes discontinuous, relationships between shots and the juxtaposition of images to create ideas not present in either one by itself.

The reasons for the development of montage were threefold:

• lack of film does not allow waste (so short shot length);
• newsreel experience – led to an understanding that images can be juxtaposed to create effects. The lack of screen time in newsreel items mitigated against smooth transitions;
• American influence.

Kuleshov wrote in 1922 of American film that it showed: 'how much plot you can get into a very short film . . . they strive to achieve the maximum number of scenes and maximum effect with the minimum waste of film . . . genuine cinema is a montage of American shots'.

Kuleshov first used the term 'montage' in 1917 in an article, *The Tasks of the Artistic Cinema*: 'regularly ordered in time and space a cinema that fixes organised human and natural raw material and organises the viewer's attention at the moment of projection through montage'. Beyond the practical reasons for montage there was also a political reason. The juxtaposition of opposing images to produce a new image paralleled the Marxist dialectic materialism where opposing forces were in conflict and ultimately produced a completely new circumstance.

The Soviet economy began to recover after the victory in the civil war. Lenin's government relaxed control of the economy to allow a necessary, if temporary, return to capitalism in the service sector. This was the 'New Economic Policy'. The opportunity came to make feature film. Kuleshov made *The Extraordinary Adventures of Mr West in the Land of the Bolsheviks* (1924). A naïve American visitor to the Soviet Union is taken in by a group of criminals who literally 'take him for a ride'. Kuleshov has not abandoned the craft he learnt with Bauer. He uses *mise en scène* carefully to create context and atmosphere (e.g. Moscow is illustrated by various tourist shots of the capital). The iconography of *Mr West* repeats the decadent motifs of Bauer's films but there is a new spirit in this film. It is quick (in every way), *cinematic* in its use of cinematography and editing to give particular elements meaning, but most of all it is an unashamedly political film.

An even more militant use of montage came with the work of Dziga Vertov and his Cine-Eye group. Vertov, his cameraman brother Mikhail Kaufman and editor wife Elizaveta Svilova bombarded the film press with manifestos (e.g. 'We', 1922) demanding that all film-makers turn their backs on drama: 'We proclaim the old films – based on the romance, theatrical films and the like – to be leprous.' The aim of cinema was to 'catch life unawares' and present a 'Communist decoding of reality'. Vertov's position reached its cinematic height with the breathtaking *Man With the Movie Camera* (1929). By that time his challenging experimental style had fallen completely out of favour with the political authorities.

By 1927 the New Economic Policy was not delivering even the slow but steady economic growth it had promised. Irritation with the lack of commercial or clear propaganda success in Soviet cinema was mounting inside the industry and amongst its political masters. Political pressure on the cinema industry became more overt with the 15th Party Congress of November 1927. The Congress's call for action, and its general tone of impatience, found a compliant response in the film industry.

The All-Union Party Conference on Cinema Affairs, which was finally held in March 1928, took a firm line. The start of the Congress was delayed due to the need for careful pre-planning, including taking reports from Party cells and trade unions within the film industry which could be relied on to fit the political leadership's need for action to outweigh the opinions of the professional élite.

As the Soviet Union celebrated the Tenth Anniversary of the Revolution (November 1927) Stalin called for the rapid strengthening of the USSR. This policy would require a quantum leap in the pace of industrialisation. All sectors of the economy would have to be focused on that one aim. A cultural revolution was required. The movies had to play their part in both illustrating and engendering that revolution.

The career of Sergei Michaelevich Eisenstein is a particularly clear exemplar of how the institution of Soviet cinema operated. Eisenstein's first two films, *Strike* (1924) and *Battleship Potemkin*

(1925), had been artistic successes and in the case of the latter a huge critical success abroad. The relative autonomy of film-makers and film organisations (of which there were many) in the 1920s meant that artistic experimentation was possible but marketing power was negligible. The films had little impact at the domestic box-office. Even during the making of his third film *October* (1927) the political atmosphere within the film industry was cooling to Eisenstein's experimentation. The film was very badly received. From then on he would have to fit his vision more closely to the whims of his political masters.

In December 1927 the 15th Party Congress agreed to the leadership's call for the collectivisation of agriculture. Eisenstein's next film *The Old & New* (released November 1929) was to be a key text in signalling the change of attitudes central to collectivisation and the industrial Five Year Plan. It is also a prime example of the institutional pressures on Soviet film-makers.

The film – long delayed and often rewritten – portrayed why and how the countryside needed to be forced into the future. Unwashed, unshaven country peasants are represented as, at best, obdurate and at worst the personification of reactionary and violent ignorance. Clean-shaven, upright representatives of the urban proletariat are portrayed as willing and able to force the peasants into the future.

Marfa the peasant heroine of the film is shown realising the error of the old rural ways when her cow dies under the strain of ploughing. She is a key figure in the demand for a dairy co-operative. The co-operative develops into a collective farm. A cow shed is built. Further development, the setting up of a winnowing machine, requires the help of urban 'workers'. The urban cadres tell the peasants, bearded and rather shabby, what to do. The peasants listen and nod accepting the superior wisdom of the worker who explains: 'We must expand the farm.'

At the end of the film Marfa returns to the countryside transformed into that most potent all Soviet icons of modernity: the tractor driver, a dramatic contrast to the destitute figure with the dead cow at the start of the film. The film ends with Marfa triumphant and empowered, inter-cut with shots of her personal and political development through the film. The final title of the film is a powerful slogan but rings hollow after the struggles that have been shown in the film that precedes it: 'And so the divisions between the city and the countryside are being erased.' Eisenstein had finally delivered the message his political masters required –

but the film still did not sit well with the simplistic orthodoxy of the party.

Boris Shumyatskii – the new political appointment at the head of the film industry – required a 'cinema intelligible to the millions'. Eisenstein was dispatched to Europe, initially to investigate sound technology. The attitude of the authorities was that if he was so popular in the west, the west could pay him. Eisenstein spent an unproductive period tied to Paramount Pictures in Hollywood. American film producers did not like him much either. After a soul destroying period in Mexico Eisenstein returned to the Soviet Union.

By 1934 all vestiges of contemporary struggle had left the cinema screens. Social, economic, political and even cinematic tensions were elided into mutual admiration under the auspices of the Stalinist hegemony. In cinema the political authorities wanted the well-made explicitness of the Vasiliev Brothers' *Chapayev* (a simple story of daring-do from the civil war). The experimentation of the 1920s, a product of particular political circumstances, no longer fitted the institutional needs.

The first Congress of Soviet Writers met in August 1934. Andrei Zhdanov – cultural commissar – announced the policy of 'Socialist Realism'. This new orthodoxy in presentation consisted of: *realnost* (realness) *idealnost* (ideology-ness) and *partiinost* (party mindedness), refrain from dialectic in form or content – simply present the struggle towards victory. Socialist Realism became in effect the Institutional Mode of Representation. In January 1935 the All-Union Creative Conference of Workers in Soviet Cinema confirmed cinema's commitment to Socialist Realist orthodoxy – dictated by political exigencies but also linked to economic imperatives external rather than internal to the film industry itself.

Eisenstein, unable to get films made in such an atmosphere, returned to teaching at the State Film School. His next feature *Bezhin Meadow* was stalled and never really finished. His historical costume drama *Alexander Nevskii* (1939) was successfully completed. It is a powerful work but contains none of the experimentation of earlier films. His film-making career ended with *Ivan the Terrible*, Part I (1942): a masterpiece, a Stalinist apologia or a rather dull bit of expressionism, depending on your view. Eisenstein died in 1948 – aged 50 – struggling to get Part II (1946) seen and/or Part III made. He died in the same year as Zhdanov, the architect of Socialist realism, and as Hollywood as he knew it shuddered (but lived to fight another day). The State he tried so hard to serve lasted another 50 years.

ITALIAN NEO-REALISM 1942–1952

Italian neo-realism is a style of film-making from the mid to late 1940s in Italy. It is typified by location shooting, the use of non-professional actors and documentary-style camera work (especially hand-held – made possible by ultra-light equipment and cameras brought over by US newsreel teams). The films themselves usually contain a politically, or at least socially, critical message. The directors most closely associated with this style are Roberto Rossellini, Luchino Visconti and Vittorio de Sica. Neo-realism is often, and indeed should be, seen as a reaction to Hollywood gloss. The movement was also a reaction to previous Italian cinema.

Italian film production developed as an outpost of the French film industry in 1905. The personnel as well as the capital was largely French. Italian production companies, particularly Ambrosio, began and thrived by utilising cheap labour and the availability of the genuine *mise en scène* of classical antiquity which encouraged high concept historical epics, e.g. *The Last Days of Pompeii* (Maggi, Italy, 1908).

In 1910 Italy was second only to France as a film exporter, concentrating on long lavish spectacles. The Italians continued to produce the same kind of product after World War I. Unfortunately, American film-makers – particularly D. W. Griffith, who had hired several Italian designers – had caught up and were capable of supplying films as visually impressive and rather better scripted. In any event Italy was in no shape to compete for the global film market. The economy had been plunged into deep economic crisis by the war. This deepening crisis also left the country open to the rise of Fascism.

Mussolini's Fascist movement came to power in 1922. The leader once described cinema as 'our best weapon of propaganda'. The Fascists – like every other European government of the inter-war years – conspicuously failed to have any effect on the film industry. There were very few 'Fascist' films. The most famous example was Alessandro Blasetti's *The Sun* (1929) which, interestingly enough, prefigured neo-realism in its use of naturalistic settings. The story of efforts to clear marshes in central Italy is one of simple hard work shot with stark simplicity.

In 1934 Luigi Freddi, the Fascist propaganda chief, was put in charge of cinema. His belief, shared by Culture Minister Bottai, was that films were for entertainment, not education. As the Fascist Government drew closer and closer to Nazi Germany the supply of Hollywood product dried up. The audiences desire for escapism was satisfied by an increase in Italian film production. This was the age of the 'cinema of distraction' of the 'white telephone era'. Films were often based in the glamorous world of show business. The beautiful people waited for that telephone to ring with news of yet another party. Glossy, big-budget productions dominated (a) because Freddi liked them and (b) because big business and government finance required the investment to be shown on screen (we can compare this to the Tradition of Quality films of post-war France – see the section on the French New Wave in this chapter).

Freddi had overseen the building of a new studio, Cinecitta (outside Rome), and the formation of a film school: Centro Sperimentale di Cinematografia. Both of these institutions became the breeding grounds for non-Fascist critics and writers, many of whom were prime movers in neo-realism, e.g. Cesare Zavattini, the scriptwriter on both of de Sica's neo-realist masterpieces *The Bicycle Thieves* (1948) and *Umberto D* (1952).

Vittorio de Sica (1902–74) started off his career in films as an actor in the 'white telephone' era. He became something of a matinée idol after *The Older Woman* (*La Vecchia Senora*) (Palermo, Italy, 1931). Through the war years he developed a reputation for directing light entertainment features such as *Rose Scarlatte* (1940) and *Teresa Venerdi* (1941). Then in 1942 came *The Children Are Watching Us*, photographed by Giusseppe Caracciolo who like de Sica was a veteran of the cinema of distraction. This film was a far more realistic look at life, using a mixture of professional and non-professional players in real locations. Some of the credit for this outbreak of realism must be given to the beginnings of a revolt against the crumbling Fascist regime. Much credit must also go to the more critical atmosphere engendered in the CSC. The uncompromising script was the work of Cesare Zavattini. After this breakthrough film came *Shoeshine* (1946) and *The Bicycle Thieves* as well as *Umberto D*.

The next film-maker to move into realist work was Roberto Rossellini (1906–77). Rossellini was very much a product of the Italian 'idle rich'. He wandered into cinema in the mid-1930s. In

1938 he achieved some measure of fame with a propaganda film *Luciano Will Be a Pilot*, which he co-scripted with his old friend Vittorio Mussolini (son of the dictator). From these inauspicious beginnings and quite possibly a sense of remorse grew a body of work including *Rome Open City* (1945), *Paisan* (1946) and *Germany Year Zero* (1947).

The third 'neo-realist' was Luchino Visconti (1906–76). Visconti, a committed Marxist from an aristocratic family, was much more sympathetic to the idea of cinema as art and conduit of ideas than his co-realists. He spent the 1930s in Paris working with Jean Renoir. In 1942 came *Obsession*, an Italian reworking of *The Postman Always Rings Twice* (filmed later by Garnett, USA, 1948), certainly dark but rather too histrionic to be described as 'realist'. In 1945 he turned to documentary realism with *Giorni di Gloria* and in 1948 he made *Terra Trema* his neo-realist film.

De Sica's *The Bicycle Thieves* is the quintessential neo-realist movie. It is a very simple story about an unemployed, working-class man in Italy in the years immediately following World War II. Finally, after years of hardship, he gets a job as a bill sticker – but only on condition that he can provide his own bicycle for the job. He manages to find just enough money to get his old bicycle out of the pawn shop. His and his family's pride is finally restored. However, as the title suggests, his bicycle is stolen, along with the prospect of his livelihood and self-respect. The main part of the film shows the man and his son's ultimately fruitless attempts to get the precious bicycle back.

The style of 'no style' is one of the characteristics of Italian neo-realism. It is of course as much of a construction of choices as any other style. The narrative structure is looser and less closed than the 'classic Hollywood film'. However, the shot composition is as carefully balanced and formal as any studio product of the 1930s and the editing style is one of careful matching and pacing. The neo-realist 'style' – like the Institutional Mode of Representation/ classic Hollywood film – gives priority to *mise en scène* – often set in real locations – over any overt cinematographic or editing technique. None the less, the camera work of the neo-realists follows the action in a hand-held documentary manner, which suggests that the subject and not the director is dictating the film, calling the shots. Sparse, naturalistic dialogue is used rather than set piece speeches. This naturalism lends itself to films that concentrate on everyday topics and the concerns of ordinary people as opposed to the glamorous or exceptional. The use of non-professional actors (rather than recognisable stars) focuses attention on the characters. Like all neo-realist films *The Bicycle Thieves* is realistic in a world weary, resigned kind of way.

Too much realism tends to be unpopular. Neo-realism – popular with non-Italian critics – was unpopular with the industry (less work for studios and actors), unpopular with governments (too critical), unpopular with the Catholic church (too morally questioning) and unpopular with audiences (too grim). In short neo-realism, the result of a particular post-Fascist mood, did not fit the institutional structures of the land of its birth.

Andreotti, the Italian Finance Minister, a ubiquitous figure in numerous Christian Democrat governments, dealt the movement a blow by withdrawing all finance for films without official approval. There would be no approval for 'political' scripts. Any films which 'slandered Italy' would not receive an export licence.

In any event, the neo-realists were moving away from the style. Visconti became engaged in opera production. Hardly less in keeping with the realist tradition was his film-making career, in which he concentrated on richly stylised adaptations of literature from *Senso* in 1954 through adaptations of Albert Camus' *The Outsider* (Italy/France, 1967) and Thomas Mann's *Death in Venice* (Italy/France, 1971) and finally *The Innocent* (Italy/France, 1976) from a novel by the proto-Fascist D'Annunzio.

After *Germany Year Zero* Rossellini abandoned the forms of neo-realism. He moved into television in the 1950s. Much of his work was in documentary but travelogues and historical biographies rather than social issues. De Sica worked with some distinction up to the time of his death as both a director and actor although increasingly on TV rather than the big screen.

In 1953 a conference was held in Parma to discuss (significantly) 'what *was* neo-realism?' De Sica and Zavattini disagreed even on a definition. The Italians seemed to care less than the French critics. Amongst the most vociferous in his praise of the movement was André Bazin – a key figure in the French 'New Wave'.

THE FRENCH NEW WAVE, 1958–1968

As neo-realism faded away in Italy a genuine movement was forming in France. The *Nouvelle Vague* or 'New Wave' consisted of a group of – initially-like minded – critics who became film-makers. They were aware of the history of their art and interested in the nature and form of that art. They delighted in making the audience aware of the artifice of film by referencing/playing with icons, forms, etc., and questioning the nature and value of film-making. All were restless artists constantly moving on and changing their responses to issues. Thus the 'movement' however brilliant was short-lived. The New Wave operated in France from 1958 to the mid-1960s.

The historical, technical, economic and social circumstances of post-war France produced a situation that could be exploited by a group of young film-makers who loved cinema, knew the rules but were not afraid to subvert them.

The term *Nouvelle Vague* was first used by Françoise Giroud in the critical journal *Cahiers du Cinéma* (1958) in discussing the 'youthful spirit' sweeping French cinema. James Monaco in *The New Wave* (1976) was very specific as to its constituents: Truffaut, Godard, Chabrol, Rohmer and Rivette. Under the influence of

The open text, *The 400 Blows* (1959). Reproduced with permission from BFI Stills, Posters and Designs

Henri Langlois and André Bazin, who were editors of *Cahiers du Cinema*, these young critics argued a new theory. Beginning with a rediscovery and re-evaluation of 'genre' pictures (see Chapter 7), the *cahiers* critics claimed that the conventions of film language (especially in *mise en scène*) proved its artistic status – all art forms have their conventions – and were an aid to creativity, i.e. working as a framework within which to express personal vision. This creative activity was the result of an 'author' (usually the director).

Thus began the *politiques des auteurs* ('auteur theory' – see Chapter 9). After writing about film through the 1950s they went on to make films. After the early 1960s they continued to make films of varying quality, but all moved away from the New Wave and certainly stopped being a 'movement'.

The New Wave was a reaction to, in Truffaut's phrase, the *'cinéma du papa'* (grandad's-cinema) of post-war France. More politely termed the 'tradition of quality', this was an established approach to film-making which was predicated upon:

- classical values
- literary scripts
- smooth cinematography
- elegant *mise en scène*.

This 'tradition' was actually quite new itself and was a direct result of the French Government's policy to foster a French – or European (and led by the French) – cinema. In the post-war period French cinema was in trouble. Economic deprivation threatened to destroy the fragile, small artisan production companies. Attempts to hold back the backlog of American product – denied to audiences for six years by the war – proved largely futile. The Government set up the CNC (the National Cinema Centre) to introduce some element of financial security and therefore confidence in the French film industry.

The CNC, via Unifrance Film, gave the industry money. Therefore the CNC wanted to see the money on the screen. The bureaucrats required lavish, cultural product. Thus the films drip in high production values and opulent studio sets, e.g. *The Gates of Night* (Carné and Prevert, France, 1946). Literary adaptations and historical epics prevailed. In short, mainstream French cinema of the 1950s is expensive but dull. Thus Truffaut in a *Cahiers du Cinéma* article of 1954 ('A Certain Tendency in French Cinema') railed against the *cinéma du papa* as too literary. Godard called it overblown and ugly, accusing it of not being 'cinema' at all. Godard believed in cinema as cinema. Not a vehicle for transmitting something else (literature) but an art in its own right with its own language/systems and aesthetics.

The *Nouvelle Vague* film-makers wanted to inject a little reality into the fairytale world of the Tradition of Quality. They pronounced the death sentence on polished, carefully scripted dialogue. Their characters' speech would be conversational and often apparently inconsequential. They were not afraid to be overtly transparent – in other words to show the working process of film-making. Thus shots could be of longer – and shorter – duration and there could be violent changes to the rhythm of cutting. The sheer existence of editing technique was no longer hidden.

Beyond the youthful desire to react against *cinéma du papa* there was a technological impetus to the *Nouvelle Vague* 'style'. In addition to the lighter cameras (see the Italian Neo-realism section in this chapter) European film-makers could also benefit from the availability of faster emulsions on film stock. There was no longer a need for powerful lights. Film-makers could go into the streets. Films became cheaper to make and film-makers became more independent. Truffaut has referred to 'a kind of euphoric ease in production'. Marrying the daughter of a rich film producer who lent him the money to set up his own production company certainly helped.

A characteristic of *Nouvelle Vague* film-makers is a lack of fear in using the open air as their *mise en scène*. Truffaut's short movie *The Brats* (1959) begins with a young woman cycling along an obviously real street into the countryside. Godard's *Breathless* begins on a dockside. Later his 'hero' meets his girl on the streets of Paris. The city goes about its business around them.

New Wave narrative structure is much looser than the Hollywood model. Not all events are clearly linked by cause and effect. Or, as Godard put it in typically extremist terms: 'a film must have a beginning, a middle and an end . . . but not necessarily in that order'. The sense of closure may not be complete. The most extreme example of this lack of closure comes at the end of Truffaut's *The 400 Blows* (1959). Having escaped from the young offenders' institution Antoine runs across a beach; having reached the sea he stops and turns to face the camera. The image freezes to capture his look of uncertainty. The viewer is left to wonder with him.

Along with Truffaut's first two features, Godard's *Breathless* (1959) is probably the best known *Nouvelle Vague* film. Godard the *enfant terrible* of the New Wave is in turns or at the same time an iconoclastic genius (steeped in film history) or a self-indulgent obscurantist. Truffaut – who fell out badly with Godard – remembered with affection a very nervous young man (from a very good family) who consumed lots of books and films (rarely finishing either), 'always very nervous and impatient', hanging around at the Cinema MacMahon which showed American movies undubbed (although he could speak no English). Godard became a critic on *Cahiers* because Bazin enjoyed his ability to shock and insult.

Breathless begins with a dedication to 'Monogram', a B-movie studio, and continues its homage to Hollywood throughout via the central character's parody of Bogart. Godard's position on Hollywood is clearly one of love and hate. The 'homage' contained within *Breathless* and later films like *A Woman Is a Woman* (1961) and *Contempt* (1963) could be seen not as celebrations so much as funeral orations.

Stylistically the film owes much to neo-realism, particularly in the use of mobile (often hand-held) cameras. Editing is much less smooth and polished than American product. Apart from the startling opening scene (discussed in Chapter 3), this is particularly well illustrated in the scene where Michel (Belmondo) visits his ex-girlfriend and steals her money. Early Godard is typified by the use of 'jump cut' (see Chapter 3). Typically, Godard had already abandoned the technique before his imitators took it on wholesale (and with less effect).

Godard's characters – even his 'hero' – are dysfunctional. New Wave central characters are typically individualistic loners and marginal to social relations. Relationships between characters are not well drawn or even explained and contextualised. Godard's use of discontinuous editing underlines this sense of separation. There is certainly plenty of action in *Breathless*, but events occur seemingly for their own sake and actions (including the final betrayal) have little or no motivation. In the final scene the spectator is left contemplating yet another misunderstanding (misreadings, misunderstandings and even grammatical errors have been a key motif through the film) as Patricia (Jean Seburg) contemplates her dead lover and asks directly to camera 'what is a "bummer?"' 'Perhaps it all is meaningless and – to use Godard's own words – cinema is simply 'a girl and a gun'.

The New Wave is not simply an interesting footnote in cinema history. Its influence lives on not least due to its impact on the 'new' cinema of the USA in the 1960s and beyond to Tarantino *et al.*

DOGME '95

It is a tribute to the possible diversity of cinema that, even in a global environment so dominated by 'Hollywood', alternatives continue to exist and at times to flourish. Thus this chapter ends with the brave – if possibly foolhardy – radical stance of a group of Danish film-makers who formed *Dogme '95* (Dogma 95). Dogma quickly moved away from a national base and its founders are wary of claiming any movement. None the less, the existence of a clearly articulated manifesto gives Dogma a clearer claim to be a movement – at least initially – than its predecessors. Some of the rhetoric brings to mind a fundamentalist sect. The movement began with a manifesto – a 'vow of chastity' no less – which certainly makes identifying characteristics easy:

I swear to submit to the following set of rules drawn up and confirmed by DOGMA 95:
1. Shooting must be done on location. Props and sets must not be brought in (if a particular prop is necessary for the story, a location must be chosen where this prop is to be found).
2. The sound must never be produced apart from the images or vice versa. (Music must not be used unless it occurs where the scene is being shot.)
3. The camera must be hand-held. Any movement or immobility attainable in the hand is permitted. (The film must not take place where the camera is standing; shooting must take place where the film takes place.)
4. The film must be in colour. Special lighting is not acceptable. (If there is too little light for exposure the scene must be cut or a single lamp be attached to the camera.)
5. Optical work and filters are forbidden.
6. The film must not contain superficial action. (Murders, weapons, etc. must not occur.)
7. Temporal and geographical alienation are forbidden. (That is to say that the film takes place here and now.)
8. Genre movies are not acceptable.

9.   The film format must be Academy 35 mm.
10. The director must not be credited.

Furthermore I swear as a director to refrain from personal taste! I am no longer an artist. I swear to refrain from creating a 'work', as I regard the instant as more important than the whole. My supreme goal is to force the truth out of my characters and settings. I swear to do so by all the means available and at the cost of any good taste and any aesthetic considerations.

Thus I make my VOW OF CHASTITY.

Copenhagen, Monday 13 March 1995
On behalf of DOGMA 95

Dogma 95 was founded by four Danish film-makers: Lars von Trier, Thomas Vinterberg, Soren Kragh-Jacobson (former rock star and already a well-known director at home) and Kristian Levring. Although naming these four as directors would immediately violate the opening salvo of their 'Manifesto' where they 'oppose the auteur concept'. They also announced their opposition to 'make-up, illusions and dramaturgical predictability'. Dogma 95 'desires to purge film so that, once again, the inner lives of the characters justify the plot'.

It is interesting that so aggressive a statement of intent should emerge form Denmark. Vinterberg has stated publicly that it is the result of Denmark being 'a small country'. Thus energy comes not only from the usual reaction to Hollywood but also to bigger neighbours like Germany. As with earlier movements there is also a technological imperative. As they put it on their official Web-site (www.dogme95.com): 'Today a technological storm is raging, the result of which will be the ultimate democratisation of the cinema. For the first time, anyone can make movies. But the more accessible the media becomes, the more important the avant-garde.'

The new digital processes, which can be used to make bigger and bolder effects movies, can also be used to make films in a more spontaneous less mannered way. It is no surprise that von Trier and Vinterberg grabbed the chance to use digital video even though it broke their own rule 9.

The Dogma group clearly positioned themselves as a new 'new wave' with references to '1960' on their website. The website declaims – perhaps only half seriously – in language which echoes the manifestos issued by Dziga Vertov's group in the 1920s:

DOGMA 95 has the expressed goal of countering 'certain tendencies' in the cinema today
DOGMA 95 is a rescue action!
In 1960 enough was enough! The movie was dead and called for resurrection. The goal was correct but the means were not! The new wave proved to be a ripple that washed ashore and turned to muck.

. . .

Predictability (dramaturgy) has become the golden calf around which we dance. Having the characters' inner lives justify the plot is too complicated, and not 'high art'. As never before, the superficial action and the superficial movie are receiving all the praise. The result is barren. An illusion of pathos and an illusion of love. To DOGMA 95 the movie is not illusion!

Von Trier had already achieved a minor international hit with *Europa* (Denmark, 1991) and some commercial success and notoriety with *Breaking the Waves* (1996), which had mixed controversial subject matter (disability, impotence, casual sex and displaced voyeurism) with a taste for jarring cinematography. *Breaking the Waves* now seems like 'Dogma-lite' or a preliminary sketch for the full-blown work *The Idiots* (1998).

On the one hand Von Trier's film is a study in embarrassment and a disturbing attack on concepts of normality and civilisation. A group of young(ish) middle-class people, disenchanted with the facile nature of the society they live in, retreat to a country house where they play at being 'spasses' (physically and mentally retarded). The 'encounter group' material does wear after a while but the strength of the film is in the group's confrontations with the straight world. Much of the action is very uncomfortable to watch. None the less, some sequences, particularly the visits to the swimming pool and a scene where Hell's Angels forget their machismo to help Jeppe go to the toilet are very moving. When two damaged characters, Jeppe and Christina, emerge from the spassing 'gang bang' to achieve tenderness and an adult relationship for the first time in their lives Von Trier achieves a kind of humanist dignity rarely seen on screen.

On the other hand Von Trier has never lost his reputation for shocking for its own sake. In the case of *The Idiots*, apart from the profoundly controversial subject matter we are confronted with clearly genuine penetrative sexual intercourse on screen. In addition, like much of Jean Luc Godard's work, *The Idiots* can be seen as embarrassingly 'badly made' (shots go out of focus, 'characters' are caught looking at the camera, etc.). Von Trier was responsible for his own intrusive cinematography. The key work on the later films (*Celebration, Mifune, Julien Donkey Boy*) is largely the responsibility of British-born Anthony Dod Mantle.

Vinterberg's *Celebration* (1998) is painful to watch because of its claustrophobic atmosphere and subject matter – a son's allegations of his father's child abuse. Many of the actors appear totally disorientated by the revelations. The resulting responses and the tensions that build are utterly gripping. What occurs on screen is so harrowing that it is possible to forget Mantle's cinematography. This fact alone is evidence that the *dogme* approach does make functional sense, both in the way it can invigorate film-making and in its suitability for certain kinds of material.

Kragh-Jacobson's *Mifune* (1999) looked much less 'rough and ready' than his colleagues' essays. Yet he stuck even closer to the dogma by using 35 mm film. His story of damaged lives and difficult decisions is rather less controversial than Vinterberg's. This may be the key to its relative lack of impact.

The dogma has spread beyond its native land as applications to film 'dogma style' were submitted to the group. Harmony Korne's *Dogma 6: Julien Donkey Boy* (1999) was an American story, about the effects of schizophrenia on a 'normal' family. Korne was no stranger to confrontational film-making as the writer of the controversial *Kids* (Clarke, US, 1995) and director of the much abused *Gummo* (1997). Dogme productions continued to accumulate. Jean-Marc Barr directed the French dogma movie *The Lovers* in 1999. Barr's film is a beautifully observed and sensitive study of a love affair between a French woman and a Yugoslavian refugee. The 'new' New Wave had returned to its spiritual home. Udo Kier, a well-known actor on television across Europe, began filming *Dogme 7 – Broken Biscuits* a German dogma film in 2000.

Jose Luis Marques – as an Argentinian – would not have been able to film in the Falklands/Malvinas without hiding his mini digital video camera. Thus he makes a benefit of hand-held cinematography. However, the film is rather slight and by titling the film *Fuckland* (Argentina, 2000) Marques provides ammunition for those critics who view *Dogme* as merely provocation.

The refreshing witty atmosphere that surrounds *Dogme* has allowed spurious rows to rage on its website and rumours to circulate of an application to film in 'dogma style' by Steven Spielberg. The vow of chastity is still attracting film-makers and encouraging new talents to seize the opportunities available for lower budget, higher content work.

The founding brotherhood continue to produce entertaining and interesting work. In a move echoing Visconti's move from realism to opera, Von Trier has already completed his musical *Dancer in the Dark* (France, 2000) – admittedly in his own idiosyncratic style. The initial tranche of Dogma was completed when the fourth founder, Levring, completed *The King is Alive* (2000). The film – shot on digital video – follows a group of disparate characters stranded in the deserts of Namibia. In true '*dogme* style' characters are given time to develop and express complexity (not least through rehearsing Shakespeare's 'King Lear'). The typical, claustrophobic atmosphere is produced by tight hand-held camera and by restricting some of the action to the broken-down bus. Levring commented on 'Dogme '95' in October 2000: 'I am not sure it will carry on. Someone is bound to come up with a new idea and a new way of doing things.' To which we must give a loud cheer for thus cinema adapts, develops and survives.

7 Genre

Nobody ever made any money out of civil war movies.
(Attributed to Sam Goldwyn on rejecting the pitch for
Gone with the Wind)

Film watchers are already aware that one of the factors which attract them to a film is its 'type'. This chapter aims to explain what factors (including music) contribute to 'type' (i.e. genre) and why we like 'typical' films. This explanation will lead to an extended reading of one genre: the Western.

In addition to the relationship between genre, authorship and star image we will also discuss the tendency to either manipulate or mix and match generic conventions in post-war cinema.

Genre simply means 'type'. Genre analysis is popular not least because it relates directly to the way that the industry works and how films are consumed. As a structure for analysis it certainly predates cinema. Dividing art forms into genres goes back as far as art does. In the study of literature genre theory was already current when Aristotle wrote his *Poetics* in the fifth century BC.

What is odd is that it took serious film criticism until the 1950s to get a grip on this most obvious of analytical tools. It is particularly odd as the film industry sold films by genre from very early days. The market for entertainment is notoriously difficult to predict. This is especially the case in a new form. Success depends on identification and capture of an audience. Genre production developed from attempts to build on initial success. Genre production also increases efficiency as you can use the same sets, writing/production teams and stars over and over again.

'Serious' genre criticism began with André Bazin, the key figure of the *Cahiers du Cinéma* (see Chapter 6). Bazin began genre study with the Western and his 1954 article 'The Western or the American film par excellence'.

Genre criticism brings the audience into the realms of film theory. The understanding of genre – whether it be by audience or critic – is predicated upon the understanding/expectation of conventions and characteristics (beyond the classic structure and sense of verisimilitude we have already discussed and which we know attract audiences). It is an advantage to film-makers and audience alike that this produces an economy of storytelling. In the opening scenes of *Stagecoach* (Ford, US, 1939) the telegraph wire is cut before a message can get through – only one word is communicated but this word is 'Geronimo', which alone conveys the genre of the film and the nature of the threat around which the narrative is structured. If we take several films from a particular genre we would expect to see similarities in a number of different areas. We can call these 'genre characteristics'.

Genre characteristics (which build upon themselves audience expectations):

- visual imagery
- plot
- character
- setting
- narrative development
- music
- stars

Genre criticism – like genre consumption and enjoyment – stresses repetition and variation not (auteur) originality. As such, analysis of genre seems exactly right for Hollywood 'factory' product, which the French critics of the *Cahiers du Cinéma* adored (at least in comparison to the home-grown *cinéma du Papa* – see Chapter 6).

Sorting films by 'genre' fits the industry model and audience consumption patterns. Yet a nagging theoretical concern does seem to leave it open to criticism/questioning. The criticism of genre criticism boils down to questions of definition, demarcation and evaluation.

To decide on the defining 'characteristics' of a genre you need to start with a provisional idea of what constitutes a genre. Andrew Tudor points nicely to the problem: 'we must first isolate the body of films which are "westerns" but they can only be isolated on the basis of the "principle characteristics" which can only be discovered from the films themselves after they have been isolated' (in B. K. Grant, *Genre Reader*, p. 71).

There are two points of contention:

1. we are moving towards a 'self-defining system' where definition and demarcation are self-perpetuating (and worse, curtail
   any questioning);
2. we can easily get caught up in an 'early form–classic–decline'
   pattern (André Bazin certainly did with reference to the Western).

One could of course reply that self-defining or not there clearly *are*
genres and maybe the 'early–classic–decline' pattern is true. The
point is – however comfortable and comforting generic forms may
be – to remain critical.

In this chapter we are using the Western as our genre case-study.
There are of course plenty more, e.g. gangster, horror, musical and
film noir. In addition there are a vast and apparently increasing
number of cross-genre films and films which take certain elements
of particular genres to make play with. It is one of the fascinations
of film history that genres and sub-genres develop and new ones
form over time.

The Western is one of the most obvious genres. It is also probably the most loved – and certainly the most hated. For lovers of
'high' art it is repetitive and naïve; for lovers of popular culture it
is direct and energetic. Both of these responses can be seen in reaction to popular film in general. Maybe it is not too fanciful to see
the Western as the quintessential and ultimately 'typical' film
genre. It is not coincidental that the 'naïve/energetic' dichotomy is
precisely the mixture of feelings with which Europe – or at least
European intellectuals – view the United States. Thus André Bazin
could claim it as 'the American film *par excellence*'.

The Western is 'American' because of its subject matter – ostensibly the formative history of the USA, specifically in the post-
Civil War period when federal government asserted its control
and the push west led to continental domination (i.e. 1865–95).
The Western has gained and secured popularity with audiences
within and outside the USA not because of any historical veracity
but through its power as myth.

The world of the screen Western is a mythology: a collection of
stories that contain a set of messages and can be utilised to
construct an identity. A mythology has to have an ideology and/or
a motivating function. Marxist or Marxian and feminist critics
would certainly argue that the Western has one (of an imperialist
teleology and patriarchy).

If the Western is in any sense history, it is generic history. Genre films refer not to the historical reality but to other genre films (and the history of the genre). This phenomenon can be illustrated by the following case-study.

The 'Western' began long before the entry of John Ford who made the genre respectable. The claim for first 'Western' – along with many other less defensible claims made by its maker – is usually attributed to Edwin S. Porter's *The Great Train Robbery* (1903) (see Chapter 4).

This film – made only five years into the history of cinema – has many of what would become recognisable genre traits of the Western. The setting is not a clearly recognisable place (e.g. Monument Valley) yet. The visual imagery is full of signifying features – icons, indeed – borrowed from the popular press of the 1890s and Wild West Shows: trains, horses, the saloon, the great outdoors and guns, of course. What *is* missing is visually signalled stock characters. There are bar girls but no 'whore with the heart of gold', a posse – but no sheriff, 'goodies' and 'baddies' – although it is not always possible to tell which is which – but no clearly discernible 'hero'.

The plot was a staple of popular literature and became so of the Western films. In a land without much law and order travel is dangerous. The 'Iron Horse', a symbol of the power – and strictures – of modernity, is held up by bandits who have already robbed the station. The tied-up station master is discovered by his daughter. She rouses the local law enforcement agents who chase, locate and shoot the robbers.

Narrative development is admittedly operating at a very basic level, but absolutely dependent on action in a way that became particularly 'Western', focusing on the conflict between the outlaws of the Wild West and the forces of law and order (expressed as a crime and chase sequence). Music would have been supplied even in 1903 for a 'silent film'. A piano would accompany the action, utilising a theatrical melodrama tradition – even early Westerns would have been accompanied by that horse rhythm, barrel-house ragtime, etc.

What is missing is a star image (still in a very early stage of development in 1903 – see Chapter 8). In addition, as we would expect for a film made in 1903 and lasting less than ten minutes, there is not much character delineation, never mind development.

Westerns from *The Great Train Robbery* onwards convey us to a particular time and place: the American frontier (or thereabouts) post-Civil War. They mythologise that time and place but it is worth remembering that the period portrayed was recent history to pre-World War I audiences in the way 'the swinging sixties' or even the height of the Cold War and the end of European empires or the Vietnam War is to present-day cinema audiences. *Stagecoach* portrayed events that would have taken place 60 years before the film was made, i.e. the same distance as World War II to us.

For Bazin *the* classic Western was *Stagecoach*. In its classic form the Western is focused very clearly on the struggle of good versus evil. In itself this struggle is of course a standard narrative trait in many genres of many art forms. Rather more particular to the Western is the relationship between law and social justice on the one hand and morality and individual conscience on the other. Invariably the latter takes the moral high ground and, at least in the case of John Ford Westerns, wins out.

In *Stagecoach* we are seduced by the excitement and personal nobility wrapped up in the American frontier myth. All the elements we saw developing in *The Great Train Robbery* are present, plus an external threat – 'Indians' (now more usually termed 'Native Americans') and a Western hero, the Ringo Kid.

Ford's career was predicated upon developing the Western as a form with *Cheyenne's Pal* (1917) through *The Iron Horse* (1924) (a film which has lately achieved silent classic status) and on to the

Mise en scène as icon: Monument Valley, *Stagecoach* (1939). Reproduced with permission from BFI Stills, Posters and Designs

miracle year of 1939 with *Young Mr Lincoln* and *Drums along the Mohawk*, as well as *Stagecoach*. He may have cut his teeth as a director on Westerns but when he set out to make Stagecoach he had not made one since *Three Bad Men* in 1926. Westerns were not perceived as quality pictures at this time. They were made quickly and cheaply and their appeal (largely to a male audience) lay in the gunfights, chases and spectacular scenery. They were B features known within the industry as 'horse operas'. In effect Ford's status as a director had risen to the point that he did not need to make Westerns anymore. He was perceived by David O. Selznick (one of the most powerful and respected Hollywood producers) as a director of quality pictures. The fact that Selznick wanted to work with Ford in 1939 clearly indicates Ford's status. The fact that Selznick pulled out when Ford insisted on making a Western indicates equally clearly the lowly status of the Western. Ford maintained his commitment to the project and was determined to make what he described as a classic Western (a term which at the time was itself contradictory). *Stagecoach* was made and the Western genre was revitalised and given a respectable status that it had not had before.

In viewing *Stagecoach*, then, it is important to consider what John Ford brought to the genre. A clue is to be found in the fact that when it was released *Stagecoach* was described in the trade press not as a Western but as a melodrama. This reflects the way in which the film focuses on people rather than gunfights and the broadening of the story to incorporate a love story and the birth of a baby (elements more likely to appeal to a female audience). The film contains all the characteristics we would expect of the genre, from the music, settings, costume and make-up through to the hero with his particularly Western code of honour, the Indian attack and the final shoot-out. The real focus, however, is character and character development. The perilous journey across the hostile Western landscape is a device that allows Ford to examine how characters interact/develop once removed from the safe confines of society and its civilised values.

John Ford certainly succeeded in his desire to a make a classic Western, if for no other reason than that critics like André Bazin consider it to be the classic example of the genre, the template from which all else was to follow. It is helpful when studying genre to have a film identifiable as a classic simply because it gives us a useful point of comparison. Comparing later Westerns to *Stagecoach*, gives us an insight into the ways in which the genre has developed.

By 1956 Ford himself was pushing the envelope of what the Western could contain with *The Searchers*. The vast epic canvas of Monument Valley still broods over the action, but the value of that action has a deep ambiguity. White men slaughter the 'Indians' too (and with some relish). A man still 'has to do' and thus Ethan (Wayne) will search for his niece for years – but with the twisted Oedipal purpose of killing her.

Ford, the American film-maker par excellence, was moving way beyond the occasionally cloying certainty of the 1948–50 'cavalry trilogy': *Fort Apache*, *She Wore a Yellow Ribbon* and *Rio Grande* (however magnificently done). Ford rather stepped back from the morally questioning stance of *The Searchers* with his final forays into directing. In *The Man Who Shot Liberty Valence* (1962) the protagonists, whilst ostensibly searching for the truth, decide to 'print the myth'.

Throughout his career Ford made other kinds of films. But they were still essentially Westerns (for more on Ford as 'auteur' see Chapter 9). On the other hand, Howard Hawks (another Hollywood stalwart) made Westerns, but they were always 'Hawks' movies. His authorial voice is as least as strong, if not stronger, than the genre characteristics of these films. He became increasingly attracted to the genre in the second half and particularly to the end of his career with *Red River* (1948), *Rio Bravo* (1959) and *Rio Lobo* (1970).

Hawks' Westerns, by the nature of their genre-twisting director and time-frame, are in a sense post-classic anyway. Perhaps *High Noon* (Zinnemann, USA, 1952) really was the last hurrah of the classic, the subplots and side issues are stripped away in this most basic of Western plots. Sheriff Kane (Gary Cooper), who has brought civilisation to the western town, has to use his own fighting skills to beat the Miller gang 'man to man'. The community leaves him to 'do what a man's gotta do', much to the chagrin of his new bride (Grace Kelly), symbolising the good and bad side of 'civilisation'.

The plot of Hawks' *Rio Bravo* mercilessly parodies this tale by having the Sheriff (John Wayne) try to avoid help from all and sundry. By the late 1950s Ford and Hawks could play within the field of the Western's basic topography. In the 1960s and 1970s Westerns moved further still into darker more ambiguous areas. We may wish to question what makes them – or even what constitutes – 'Westerns' by the time of *Left Handed Gun* (Penn, 1958). Paul Newman stars as 'Billy the Kid', utilising 'method' acting to explore the tragic nature of the character. One cannot imagine John Wayne following that route. Penn went on to direct *Bonnie and Clyde* (1967) – in many ways an updated 'amoral' Western – and *Little Big Man* (1970). The latter is a major contender for the title of first 'revisionist' Western. Its overt questioning of the veracity of the Western 'myth' predates *Unforgiven* (Eastwood, USA, 1992) by two decades.

Robert Altman's *McCabe and Mrs Miller* (1971) has all the right elements of *mise en scène* but is shot in a washed-out manner, reminiscent of old photographs. The plot development lacks the Western's usual vitality and replaces it with world-weary cynicism. Altman went on to direct his own 'revisionist' Western *Buffalo Bill and the Indians* in 1976. The film mercilessly exposes the façade of the Wild West Show that gave the Western much of its iconography and subject matter.

In the 1960s and 1970s Sam Peckinpah redesigned Westerns and brought to them an authorial voice as strong as Ford's or Hawks'. Peckinpah's directing career began on TV with 'The Rifleman'. His affair with the movie Western began with *Guns in the Afternoon (Ride the High Country)* in 1962. Randolph Scott (himself an iconic figure in earlier Westerns) and Joel MacRae star as old-timers struggling with the new civilisation.

Peckinpah's work (not only in Westerns) developed into baroque variations on the basic riff of testing personal honour, values and codes, with such films as *Pat Garrett and Billy the Kid* (1973) and *Bring Me the Head of Alfredo Garcia* (1974). His finest (Western) moment came with *The Wild Bunch* (1969).

The setting for *The Wild Bunch* is perfectly Western: border territory in the late nineteenth century. The milieu of visual imagery and non-diegetic music are unmistakably 'Western'. The plot is the basic 'caper gone wrong', beloved of the genre from *The Great Train Robbery* onwards. However, the narrative development and character motivation is as dark and complex as that in *The Searchers* but presented in a much more unflinching and knowing manner. There is a sense of professionalism displayed by the characters *but* any 'heroism' is immediately undermined by William Holden's opening line during the bank raid: 'If they move . . . kill 'em.' There is no happy ending for these strong men – no life of repose with Dallas (the heroine of *Stagecoach*) – all end in a fight to the (literal) finish. Is this a 'post-Western'? Is it the West seen through Mexican eyes – or under the influence of Borges (who is, according to David Thomson in *Biographical Dictionary of Film*, a huge fan)?

In the 1960s and 1970s the genre was going through a period of transition where 'proper' Westerns seemed to all but disappear. Yet the Western's influence was undimmed. Perhaps the biggest and most successful Western of them all is *Star Wars* (Lucas, USA, 1977). *Star Wars* presents us with a narrative that has many Western characteristics, most powerfully in the character and motivation of Luke Skywalker, who like Ethan in *The Searchers* returns to the burnt-out homestead of his family and, motivated by a desire for revenge, takes the law into his own hands. This is not the only reference to Ford's film. The saloon bar where we first encounter Han Solo looks almost exactly like the bar in *The Searchers* where Ethan learns of Cicatrice (in spite of its more exotic-looking occupants). Han Solo himself displays many of the characteristics of the Western hero. He is skilful with his weapons, which in true Western fashion he wears in a gun belt and holster. He has, to say the least, a dubious relationship with the forces of law and order, and the rough-bitten cynicism that we associate with characters like Ethan (although his character is not so dark). In spite of these examples most of the *mise en scène* of *Star Wars* clearly belongs to the science fiction genre but even in the elaborate space sets there is an echo of the Western. American heroes are still battling it out on the frontier – it's just that the frontier has expanded from the West to space.

As all sense of certainty in the genre disappeared the flame was kept alive on TV, particularly via the simple values of series such as *Bonanza* and *Rawhide*. The latter (1959–66) starred one Clint Eastwood. Towards the end of his *Rawhide* career Eastwood was persuaded to take the lead part in Sergio Leone's *A Fistful of Dollars* (1964). After the surprising success of this Spaghetti Western, Eastwood went on to star in *For a Few Dollars More* (1966) and *The Good, the Bad and the Ugly* (1967). Leone's 'Westerns' have all the elements we would expect from the genre. The visual imagery – guns, horses, spurs – is so typical as to be parodic. These films are driven by Ennio Morricone's spare musical scores – all gunshots and whoops. The setting is the harsh frontier (admittedly filmed in Spain), dated precisely in the classic post-Civil War period. The plots revolve around revenge and the need for 'what a man's gotta do', and narrative development is entirely through action (usually a shoot-out).

Eastwood made the journey from the 'impure' and possibly even camp form of Spaghetti Western – via working with Don Siegal and *Dirty Harry* (1971) – into direction and a return to a more American and, indeed, serious form of Western with *High Plains Drifter* (1973), *The Outlaw Jose Wales* (1976) and *Pale Rider* (1985). The genre itself achieved a certain resurgence through a wave of 'revisionism' fed by new American historians. *Dances with Wolves* (Costner, US, 1990) is positioned precisely in the post-Civil War era. It is closely related to the Ford epics *Stagecoach* and *The Searchers* – not least in the strong sense of personal (rather mawkish) morality and worthiness of its material.

With *Unforgiven* (1992) Eastwood himself begins to question the machismo of much of his earlier work, primarily through the reformed outlaw William Munny, who is persuaded back to do one last job. The film raises questions about the nature of violence and murder. This is no longer the straightforward world where 'a man's gotta do' but a place of moral ambiguity, darkness and uncertainty where the hero shows fear of death as well as remorse for his conduct. Eastwood's achievement is that he is able to take the genre in new directions by raising such questions, whilst at the same time conforming to the characteristics of the genre and fulfilling audience expectations. There are still clear problems with the representation of women who, apart from Munny's dead wife, are all whores. Their place in the narrative is, however, more significant. It is their refusal to simply accept maltreatment that kick-starts the whole story. This prefigures perhaps, the radical representation of women in *Bad Girls* (Kaplan, 1994), where the whores themselves are actively on the run from civilisation, or *Ballad of Little Joe* (Greenwald, 1993 USA), where a woman escaping the civilised values of the east 'out-toughs' the frontier men. It should be noted there is a tradition of women-centred Westerns, but in this sub-genre the women are the problem the man has to 'solve', e.g. in *Annie Get Your Gun* (Sidney, 1950) it is Betty Hutton and in *Calamity Jane* (Butler, 1953) it is Doris Day. These tough girls are both wooed by singing star Howard Keel.

The development of the genre continued. In 1990 Kevin Costner had attempted to suture in a native American view of the west, totally revising the way in which the conflict between white and native Americans had previously been represented. Similarly, in 1993 Mario van Peebles in *Posse* gave us black cowboys (previously seen as comic or incongruous figures, e.g. *Blazing Saddles* (Brookes, 1974)). Ang Lee – the master of revisiting diverse genres – took on the Western with *Ride with the Devil* (1999), which is in the correct historical period, looks and sounds like a Western but reads like a brat pack teen-angst movie.

Since Ford wrote the rule book – and Hawks (and possibly Ford) undermined its certainties – anything and everything has been poured into the Western container at one time or another, as is illustrated by the examples above. So we may well ask: what is left of 'the Western'? What remains in these revised, even in parody, Westerns is the iconography.

'Icon' is a word that is used rather too often and without definition. An icon – from its origins in the Orthodox Church – is an image given (by whatever means) cultural and historical resonance. We (the audience, congregation, etc.) have to be able to read them and they feed our expectations. Icons carry messages and values. They are literally significant so they can be moved and *keep their significance*.

Ed Buscombe in several intelligent and sensitive pieces of genre analysis has identified the iconography of the Western in the clothing and, in particular, the hardware, especially the six-gun. Part of the iconography of the movies is the people in them. Thus by repetition/reputation and reinforcement almost *any* film with John Wayne – or indeed Clint Eastwood – in it is capable of being read as a Western. These stars (see next chapter) are performers whose 'image' feeds back into future performances. To whole generations of film-goers and TV watchers Clint is a cowboy. Invariably he gives that audience what they want.

In conclusion, genre works by fulfilling audience expectations. This means that genre films must have elements that are expected, predictable and formulaic (see the list of genre characteristics in this chapter). We buy the tickets because we know what we are going to get. We have already developed a liking for the 'type' and yet, in spite of having clearly defined expectations of what a genre film must do, we want each one to be different. This means that the film-makers must tread a fine balance between providing us with the predictable elements of the genre whilst still managing to do something fresh and interesting. As Eastwood himself put it (*Time Out*, 1992), the Western is 'a genre in which you can analyse new subject matter and moralities, you can take it in different directions'. Does this deny the existence of Westerns? No – it simply underlines the structuring and attractive power of this 'the American movie *par excellence*' (Bazin).

The critics of the French New Wave – including André Bazin – contended that the great American auteurs (as they saw them) Ford and Hawks succeeded in simultaneously working within the genre and overcoming its limitations by placing a personal stamp on their films.

Whether we are looking at Westerns or any other genre the point of interest is not merely to list the genre characteristics but to look at how the film handles the balance/tension between predictability and originality. A simple but effective approach to the study of genre films is to ask two questions:

- What aspects of this film are predictable and formulaic?
- What aspects of this film are surprising, original or different?

The pleasure of the text lies in the way the film handles the balance between these two equally necessary things.

8 Stardom

'People' . . . I ain't 'people'. I am a – a shimmering glowing star
in the cinema firmament.
(Lina Lamont (Jean Hagen) declaiming her status in *Singing
in the Rain* (Kelly, 1952))

Stardom is numinous, glamorous, intangible yet keenly felt. It
seems to be a natural, even primordial, force in film. Yet an enormous amount of effort goes into creating this force. In the classic
Hollywood period (see Chapter 5) major 'movies' were almost
exclusively sold on star image. Thus the actor – and just as often
the actress, was monarch, even dictator.

Bill Daniels gained his reputation as a director of photography
(after many years of sterling work beginning with Von Stroheim's
Foolish Wives in 1922) because he was 'Garbo's cinematographer'.
She insisted on being photographed by him in such MGM star
vehicles as *Queen Christina* (Mamoulian, 1933), *Anna Karenina*
(Brown, 1935) and *Ninotchka* (Lubitsch, 1939). Charles Lang took
over from Lee Garmes as Marlene Dietrich's favoured photographer after he gained her approval by simply over-lighting her (120
candles) as compared to the rest of the set and other actors including Gary Cooper (100–10 candles) in *Desire* (Borzage, 1936). The
effect of such lighting is to create a luminous and numinous aura
of glamour around the star.

Stardom is certainly at least partially to do with looking good
on screen – but it has to be more. In order to investigate this most
important and 'indefinable' of phenomena we must attempt a
typology focused on twin factors:

- What constitutes a star?
- What does a star do?

The functional definition of a 'star' is clearly put by John Ellis in C. Gledhill (ed.) *Star Signs* (London, 1992): 'a performer in a particular medium whose figure enters into subsidiary forms of circulation and then feeds back into future performances'. Richard Dyer has made major contributions to theorising the star via two seminal studies: *Stars* (1980) and *Heavenly Bodies* (1986). For Dyer the star image has four components:

- what the industry puts out;
- what the media say;
- what the star says and does;
- what the audience or spectator selects.

NB: only one component of the four is actually produced by the star. Star status is to some extent produced by both fans and the star themselves but needs to be authenticated in other media. Dyer also notes that stars are very much players in intertextuality – their image is taken from and beyond them and used by the industry and the audience. Thus the 'star image' is powerful enough to be moved from context to context and yet unstable enough to be used in different ways (see Chapter 10 for a discussion of the audience and the spectator).

Christine Gledhill, in *Stardom: The Industry of Desire* (1991), puts forward a view that stars reach the audience primarily through their bodies. This leads to a need to 'keep up appearances' and a short screen life for women. In addition to valuable work on the psychology of stardom and star reception, Gledhill has given all 'star gazers' a pithy taxonomy of the star as a construct of:

- real person
- 'reel' person
- 'star persona'.

It is crystal clear that stars sell movies. The question is how do they do so. What does a star actually do

- within the movie
- within the movie business
- in the wider world of the audience?

'Stars' – i.e. clearly identified, commodified and marketed individuals – were first used by the film industry in France (by the

Film d'Art in 1907–08). Florence Lawrence was named 'The Biograph Girl' and became the first US film star in 1910. Mary Pickford and Charlie Chaplin took the concept to commercial heights (never exceeded since) in the years before, during and after the First World War.

In the classical Hollywood era there was a close and mutually beneficial relationship between genre and star (see previous chapter). Stars were often linked to a genre by the studios. This was a useful device in building a star 'image' (e.g. Wayne as a cowboy) and allowed for synergy in marketing. It was typical of a playful master like Hitchcock that he could succeed in using such big stars as James Stewart (in *Rear Window* (1954) and *Vertigo* (1958)) and Cary Grant (in *Notorious* (1946)) playing against 'type'.

Stars – once they have achieved fame – never like being confined to a genre. Attempts to break out often lead to disappointment; e.g. Sylvester Stallone's performance in *Copland* (Mangold, US, 1997) was creditable but the commercial failure of the film shows the power of the star image. The audience did not wish to overcome its connection with the image of Stallone as an honest action-man and therefore couldn't accept him as a fat and inadequate cop.

The 'star' functions within the industry and within the narrative, stimulating (creating?) our desires and fantasies. How each star does that (and how each star is consumed) is an interesting and fruitful area of analysis. The question of how stardom is constituted is also rather rich, complicated and necessarily individual. None the less we can develop a typology of stardom via an investigation of stars themselves. We will investigate two such figures from the 'cinema firmament': Marilyn Monroe and Tom Cruise.

MARILYN MONROE

It is most appealing to investigate Monroe via her biography and contribution to subsidiary forms of communication. After all, most of her posthumous fan base have done precisely that. None the less we should never forget that stardom itself is predicated upon the film career and her 'star' contribution to her movies. It is also important to see how 'Marilyn Monroe' is consumed. Stardom is such a powerful, attractive force it needs to be 'read' in relation to intended and actual responses and 'uses' (which may be less fixed than the producer/director or even star may expect or indeed want).

Marilyn Monroe was born Norma Jean Baker on 1 June 1926, in Los Angeles, California, USA. She was a Hollywood child. Her mother was a film-cutter at RKO. Norma's father rode off on his motorbike and abandoned the family. Her mother drifted into a number of disastrous casual relationships and experienced a breakdown and the child was taken into care, where she was allegedly both physically and sexually abused. She married at sixteen to James Dougherty (whom she called 'Daddy'). After some modelling success Norma Jean, like so many Los Angeles girls, went to the Actors' Lab in Hollywood. She started using the name 'Marilyn Monroe' in 1946, but did not legally change it until 1956.

Her first film appearance was in 1947 with a bit part in *The Shocking Miss Pilgrim* (Seaton, USA, 1947) starring Betty Grable. A better role came as Evie in *Dangerous Years* (Pierson, USA, 1947). In 1948, Twentieth Century Fox failed to renew her contract so she went back to modelling and acting school. Columbia gave her a contract and she appeared in a number of undistinguished B-movies. In 1949 Marilyn appeared in a United Artists Marx Brothers vehicle, *Love Happy* (Miller, USA, 1949), and posed nude for the shot that was later – with the approval of Monroe's advisors – to appear in *Playboy* magazine (Christmas 1953). David Thomson – acute as always – notes in *A Biographical Dictionary of Film* (1995) that the still images are the most powerful: 'Her fame increases, and as it does so we see how far she depended on, and excelled in, photographs – not movies. She gave great still.'

In 1950 Marilyn appeared in five films. A small part (as Angela Phinlay) in John Huston's *Asphalt Jungle* was her big break. She was spotted by Joseph Mankiewicz. He directed her (along with Bette Davis *et al.*) in *All About Eve*. Monroe was back at Fox. A star analysis requires us to ask: 'What was Monroe contributing to these films as a performer?' We could easily concur with David Thompson that in the early films we get 'the archetypal forlorn starlet' but also the rather more interesting 'versions of the sexual careerist protected by an older and wiser man'. Admittedly this is Thompson projecting his own responses (and his reading of her personality) very large. There is something rather more touching – and therefore rather more commercially valuable – there too: 'Monroe' is both beautiful (therefore an object of aspiration) and vulnerable (therefore an object of sympathy).

Marilyn Monroe 'stars' in *Gentlemen Prefer Blondes* (1953). 20th Century Fox (courtesy Kobal)

In 1951, Marilyn got a bigger role in *Love Nest* (Newman, USA, 1951). In the following year Marilyn appeared alongside Cary Grant and Ginger Rogers in *Monkey Business* (Hawks, USA, 1952) as Lois Laurel – a platinum blonde. In 1953 *Niagara* (Hathaway) with Joseph Cotton and *Gentlemen Prefer Blondes* (another film directed by Howard Hawks) made her a star. Her move to the big league was confirmed as she appeared (as Angela Phinlay) with top billing above Betty Grable and Lauren Bacall in *How to Marry a Millionaire* (Negulesco, USA, 1953). Billy Wilder's *The Seven Year Itch*, released in 1955, created Monroe's iconic moment: she stops over the air-conditioning grate and the draught lifts her dress in a symbol of free sexuality that has become part of Western culture. Her universal yet undervalued status was signalled by her character being labelled 'the girl'. The mixture of extraordinary sexual magnetism coupled with apparent ignorance of the true meaning of her effect on observers was never seen to better effect than in this film. After *The Seven Year Itch* much of her work (including with *Some Like it Hot* with Wilder) is parody.

Marilyn was suspended by Fox for not reporting for work on a dreadful Betty Grable vehicle *How to Be Very Popular* (Nunnally, USA, 1955). Her professional reputation had begun to take a slide. Her personal life continued to fascinate the world. In 1955 she married and divorced baseball player Joe Dimaggio.

By 1955 Monroe was much more (and less) than a movie actress. She had begun her full-time affair with the publicity apparatus which has continued beyond her death. Her on-screen performances became less and less the point of attention as the disruptions to her career became more and more fascinating to the media.

Monroe tried to move away from the stereotype of the 'dizzy blonde' via 'method acting' with Lee Strasberg, psychoanalysis, a serious role as Cherie in *Bus Stop* (Logan, USA, 1956) and marriage to Arthur Miller. *The Prince and the Showgirl* (Olivier, UK/US, 1957) was made in England with Britain's finest thespians, in a co-production between Monroe and Warner Brothers no less. The film was meant to cement her position as a serious actress. However, during filming drink and drugs problems were becoming more obvious. Her behaviour on and off set was less than professional. After a year's rest Marilyn returned as 'Sugar Kane (Kowalczyk)' in *Some Like it Hot* (Wilder, USA, 1959) with Tony Curtis and Jack Lemmon.

Monroe still looked great on screen. The fact that she looked rather blank would not have diminished her allure. However, personal problems had made filming very difficult. A year later she managed to complete *Let's Make Love* (Cukor, USA, 1960) but work on *The Misfits* (Huston, USA, 1961) was delayed due to medical problems. The film would prove to be the final bow for Clark Gable, who would die later that year of a heart attack. Monroe was sacked from George Cukor's *Something's Got to Give* in which she would have starred with Dean Martin. The film was never completed. On August 5 1962, aged 36, Monroe died of a drug overdose in the city of her birth and fame, Los Angeles, California, USA.

Monroe's reputation was made in only 30 films – many of which in the early days were bit parts and/or in very poor pictures indeed. Many of the later ones were rather undistinguished too. Yet, the licensing of Marilyn's name and likeness nets the Monroe estate more than $2 million a year. The amount of money expended on pirate merchandise can only be guessed at. Hundreds of items of Monroe memorabilia were auctioned off at Christies in late October, 1999. The gown she wore to serenade President Kennedy at his birthday celebrations in 1961 was sold for over $1 million.

In 1995 the readers of *Empire* magazine voted Monroe as second (behind Harrison Ford) of the '100 Sexiest Stars in Film History'. She was ranked eighth in the same magazine's 'Top 100 Movie Stars of All Time' poll in October 1997. In 1999 she could still be named the 'Number One Sex Star of the 20th Century' by *Playboy* magazine (having appeared on the first cover in 1953). In the same year she was voted 'Sexiest Woman of the Century' by *People* magazine. She continues to make film appearances as an iconic image caught in archive footage, e.g. in *The Front* (Ritt, USA, 1976) and *L.A. Confidential* (Hanson, USA, 1997). These posthumous appearances confirm her status and a star image which was already frozen in time even briefly after her death, e.g. in *The Love Goddesses: A History of Sex in the Cinema* (Ferguson, USA, 1965).

What is Monroe's appeal? Perhaps the answer is what links the above phenomena – and what links them to the material from and around her career. Sex and stardom for 'Monroe' were and remain clearly linked. Most analysts would agree that the packaging of female stars has focused on sexual stereotypes: virgins, vamps or goddesses. Monroe's iconography is certainly one of (sexual) availability: the pout, the clinging dress, the billowing skirt.

'Monroe' imagined as 'blonde bombshell' sex symbol is invariably described as an 'icon'. As we noted in the previous chapter, 'icon' is a word that needs to used with care. The images that deserve the epithet must have been given cultural and historical resonance and we have to be able to read them. Monroe becomes a symbol – for sex.

Icons are in themselves significant so they can be moved and keep their significance. 'Monroe' is such a powerful image that it can be transferred not only by the star herself across films and in subsidiary forms but also by other artists. The examples of 'borrowing' the Monroe iconography can be seen in such diverse artistic practices as the Andy Warhol portrait, the use of a Monroe-like ingenue image by actresses such as Theresa Russell (who played the Monroe clone 'actress' in *Insignificance* (Roeg, 1985)) and the manipulation of the image in much of the work of Madonna, e.g. the 1989 video for 'Material Girl'. Of course this borrowing of the image ultimately reinforces its iconic power.

'Monroe' is able to transcend the merely sexual by factoring in the enduring power of tragedy. Thus Monroe becomes a simulacrum of tragedy, vulnerability and sex (or from a darker point of view, we enjoy the thrill of *schadenfreude*, power, jealousy and hypocrisy). Thus it was entirely consistent with the Monroe image – and the iconic nature of stardom itself – that in 1997 the song Elton John wrote for Monroe, 'Candle in the Wind', was revived for the ceremonies that marked the passing of Princess Diana.

Monroe can be used as a projection for any individual, particularly a showbiz wannabe, of glamour mixed with thwarted ambition and a splash of self-pity. Monroe herself gave her fans the required texts, i.e. through 'the subsidiary forms'. For example in a 1957 *People* magazine interview:

My problem is that I drive myself . . . I'm trying to become an artist, and to be true, and sometimes I feel I'm on the verge of craziness, I'm just trying to get the truest part of myself out, and it's very hard. There are times when I think, 'All I have to be is true'. But sometimes it doesn't come out so easily. I always have this secret feeling that I'm really a fake or something, a phony.

Or, in more mawkish mode, in 1960: 'No one ever told me I was pretty when I was a little girl. All little girls should be told they're pretty, even if they aren't.' In 1961 the personal psycho/melodrama is unbearable: 'I knew I belonged to the public and to the world, not because I was talented or even beautiful, but because I never had belonged to anything or anyone else.'

Monroe was also an individual who (publicly) relished yet feared the power of stardom. Early quotes like: 'I want to be a big star more than anything. It's something precious.' And 'There was my name up in lights. I said "God, somebody's made a mistake!" But there it was in lights. And I sat there and said, "Remember, you're not a star." Yet there it was up in lights' are countered with: 'It scares me. All those people I don't know, sometimes they're so emotional. I mean, if they love you that much without knowing you, they can also hate you the same way.'

The Monroe tragic mystique is enhanced by and tied to her links with the Kennedy clan. As a lover of both John and Robert she is forever part of the iconography of the post-war decades and in particular of the mythology of sudden, tragic and public death. A Hollywood website which sells fake driving licences of the famous advertises itself using three names: Elvis, Marilyn and Diana.

At her death Laurence Olivier summed up the 'Monroe as tragic heroine' position: 'She was the victim of ballyhoo and sensation – exploited beyond anyone's means.' The almost parodic presentation of female sexuality combined with tragic life story have produced some most interesting responses to 'Monroe' from audiences post-Monroe. A browse through the websites lovingly set up and maintained by fans of Marilyn (as she is usually personalised on these sites) gains even the casual observer a fascinating glimpse into a subculture.

'Marilyn Monroe – The Definition of Beauty' allows fans to 'pay homage to "the most beautiful woman ever"'. Several sites use the term 'shrine' (second only to the term 'icon' in its popularity). Many sites positively solicit photographs, art works *in memorium* and (maudlin) poems. Several sites feature 'look-alikes'. Many 'actresses' and 'artists' seem unable to resist impersonation as well as veneration of their idol. The text drips glamour and tragedy. The vast majority of the sites are run by men. These sites often celebrate an interesting twist on the use of Marilyn's sexual persona i.e. the 'look-alikes' are male. Clearly this 'queering' of 'Monroe' goes well beyond the preferred reading offered by the studios.

A wide range of consumers, well beyond her fanatical fan base, have used the Monroe legacy and iconography to explore or contribute to their personal identity. This illustrates the fact that the meanings and responses generated by performers and the use of star image by those other than the star are potentially much less fixed than film industry executives imagine.

TOM CRUISE

Cruise as a more recent star is an interesting parallel to Monroe, not least in the power of stardom to gain auteur status. Big stars have always had power – especially in Hollywood. However, this power was exerted in terms of look, e.g. 'pet' cinematographers, or ridiculous demands for 'star treatment', e.g. Gloria Swanson rather missing the point of *Sunset Boulevard* (Wilder, 1949) and being brought on set in a sedan chair. Big stars in the late twentieth/early twenty-first century have become rather more businesslike.

Thomas Cruise Mapother IV was born on 3 July (only hours early for Independence Day) 1962 in Syracuse, New York, USA. For a decade, as Tom Cruise, he has been the top earner in Hollywood. His salary for *Mission Impossible II* (Woo, USA, 2000) was $20 million. As a 14-year-old his ambition was to become a priest. By that time, due to a dysfunctional family background, he had attended 15 different schools. He finally settled in Glen Ridge, New Jersey, with his mother and a new stepfather. He took up acting after losing his place on his high school wrestling team. As his interest in acting took hold he abandoned his plans of becoming a priest, dropped out of school, and at age 18 headed for New York. He made his film debut with a small part in *Endless Love* (Zeffirelli, US, 1981) and became first a minor league 'star' with films like *All the Right Moves* (Chapman, USA,1983) and *Risky Business* (Brickman, USA, 1983) and then very quickly a very big star with some of the top grossing films of the 1980s: as Lieutenant Pete 'Maverick' Mitchell in *Top Gun* (Scott, USA,1986); as Charlie Babbitt in *Rain Man* (Levinson, USA,1988) and Ron Kovic *Born on the Fourth of July* (Stone, USA, 1989) as well as a barn-storming performance as Vincent in Martin Scorsese's *The Color of Money* (1986). The latter pair of films showed that Cruise was also capable of doing difficult 'proper' work in a way that Monroe, for example, was never allowed to do.

Cruise's contribution as performer to the films of the 1980s can be summed up in one word: energy. He may be small. His smile might be slightly lopsided. Although that smile has become a star sign in itself. This point was perfectly made when in *MI:2* arch-criminal Sean Ambrose comments that the most annoying thing about 'Ethan Hunt' is his grin. Cruise might not always play glamorous roles. None the less, his on-screen persona is one of almost hyperactivity. The 'boy next door but well scrubbed and with a twinkle in his eye' looks made him a sure-fire idol as soon as he got the right part, i.e. *Top Gun*. The fact that he could transfer this winning smile and energising presence into much more interesting and challenging work is a tribute to his talent – but also to the enduring power of his 'star image'.

In 1990 he renounced his Catholic beliefs and embraced the Church of Scientology, claiming that Scientology had cured him of dyslexia. He married actress Nicole Kidman on Christmas Eve 1990 (having divorced Mimi Rogers). The couple adopted two children (Isabella and Connor). In the 1990s Cruise became the highest paid actor in the world, earning an average 15 million dollars per appearance. Almost all of the high concept (i.e. glossy) high-profile movies he made were huge box-office hits. They include: *Days of Thunder* (Scott, USA, 1990), *Far and Away* (Howard, USA, 1992) with his wife, *A Few Good Men* (Reiner, USA, 1992) with Jack Nicholson and *The Firm* (Pollack, USA, 1993). These were popular movies but not 'great films'. Cruise the actor wanted more and thus accepted the part of bisexual vampire Lestat de Lioncourt in Neil Jordan's art-house/box-office cross-over *Interview with the Vampire: The Vampire Chronicles* (1994). Cruise also starred as Ethan Hunt in *Mission Impossible* (De Palma, USA, 1996). It was a shrewd move to take a percentage of the gross of the movie. It has yielded him a total of $70 million. *Jerry Maguire* (Crowe, USA, 1996) gained Cruise an Academy Award Nomination for best actor.

His reputation as a 'serious' actor was confirmed with performances as Doctor William 'Bill' Harford in Kubrick's *Eyes Wide Shut* (1999) and as Frank T. J. Mackey in *Magnolia* (Anderson, US,1999). Both engagements were performed for well under his usual salary bill and in Kubrick's case for rather longer than expected – but by then the royalties for *Mission Impossible* were flowing and the cheque for *MI2* was in the post.

In 1990 Cruise was voted *People* magazine's 'Sexiest Man Alive'. In 1995 readers of *Empire* magazine voted him as number 41 of the '100 Sexiest Stars in Film History'. In October 1997 he came in at number three in the same magazine's 'Top 100 Movie Stars of All Time' list and was chosen by *People* magazine as one of the 50 most beautiful people in the world.

'Tom Cruise' (i.e. the star image of Mr Mapother) is a beautiful person. Humble, kind, able to overcome disability. In 1996 he stopped to help a hit and run victim and paid her hospital bills. The victim turned out to be an aspiring Brazilian actress who was keen to publicise the event. While he was working with Paul Newman on *The Color of Money* the older actor engaged him in political discussions. Cruise experienced a profound change in outlook and, appalled by his previous involvement in jingoistic gloss like *Top Gun*, he chose to star in *Born on the Fourth of July*. In 1998 he received the John Huston Award for Artists Rights. Cruise and Kidman have donated to Hillary Clinton's campaign for a seat in the US Senate. This was a thinking, serious – as well as seriously rich – young couple.

Cruise – as the brightest star in today's 'cinema firmament' – is a major figure on the websites that exploit his star image, ranging from the shamelessly commercial (never a shortage of Tom Cruise-related items at this popular auction house) through the strangely opportunist (a Hollywood hair products company offers: 'Tom's hair secrets revealed') to hundreds of touchingly earnest sites of veneration. Many, many of these latter sites are the work of (ostensibly) teenage girls. Their only desire appears to be to post pictures and gossip about the object of their desire. 'Worship' is a term which recurs often. These fans are fiercely loyal to the star's image. Theirs is an unselfish love. Their devotion to Kidman is remarkable. Any suggestions that this was a less (or more) than perfect marriage – including the rumours of homosexuality – are as robustly damned by the fans as by Mr Cruise and his lawyers.

Cruise's fan base seems very happy to consume at face value the meanings and responses generated by the performer as fixed by film producers, casting directors and Cruise himself: thoughtful, talented but still very much the action man/movie star. His public persona stresses his love of – as well as Nicole and the kids – skydiving, scuba diving, and piloting his private stunt plane. Much of the pre-publicity for *MI2* – which included a stunning trailer/website featuring Tom dangling from a cliff – played up the rumour that he did all of his own stunts. John Woo, director of *MI2*, was only too happy to comment on that numinous thing that is stardom: 'When he talks, he has so much energy it's almost like he's dancing. So I used that to choreograph his action scenes.'

That Woo was given the *MI2* director's chair on the initiative of Cruise, advised by John Travolta, is evidence of the star as the creative force behind the movie, i.e. 'the author' (or *auteur*). The power of stardom has led some critics to allow the star a centrally creative position within the film-making process. Thus stardom enters the realm of auteur (authorship) theory. The next chapter will confront the controversial issue of authorship in the cinema.

Tom Cruise plays 'Tom Cruise', *Mission Impossible 2* (2000). Paramount (courtesy Kobal)

9 Auteur

Whether you like it or not, you are.
> (Martin Scorsese (*Projections* 4, 1996))

What was I trying to achieve ? . . . a cheque
> (John Ford in interview with a French journalist, 1967)

This chapter will answer several key questions:

* What is auteur theory?
* How did it develop?
* What does it tell us about the way films are made?

In the 1950s the young writers of the *Cahiers du Cinéma* (see Chapter 6) argued a new theory: *politiques des auteurs*. This position began the critical tradition of 'auteur theory'. Auteur theory was born out of twin passions: a love of Hollywood product combined with a desire to raise film to the status of a unique art form. They argued a position that film's generic ideas produced creative conventions in cinema language which could then be exploited and developed by individual artists (auteurs) into a personal vision.

The *Cahiers* position was expressed clearly by the magazine's editor André Bazin in 1957 when he wrote of 'choosing in the artistic creation the personal factor as a criterion of reference, and then postulating its permanence and even its progress from one work to the next'.

Talk of artistic creation and the term 'auteur' (author) placed the director (and not the script-writer) centrally as the author of the film. The director 'wrote' in pictures. This position was a development of that taken by the critic and film-maker Alexandre Austruc who had written in 1948 of 'le camera stylo'. The *politiques des auteurs* was seized upon by the young *Cahiers* writers, e.g. Truffaut and Godard in their war against the literary *cinéma du papa* of post-war France.

If the film-maker was to be seen as author they would have to exhibit through a series of films clear 'auteur' characteristics:

- visual style – mise en scène and cinematography;
- narrative structure and features;
- particular character traits/situations;
- sets of themes.

These characteristics will be clearly seen in all of an auteur's work (in whatever genre). Truffaut's favourite candidate for auteur status was Alfred Hitchcock. Hitchcock's themes are clear enough: crime and suspense. His characters are driven by guilt, obsession and a fair sprinkling of phobias. His narrative structure is one of flawed characters driven by circumstance, e.g. Bruno (Robert Walker) in *Strangers on a Train* (1951) or Scotty (James Stewart) in *Vertigo* (1958). The narrative builds to a denouement, often via false climaxes and waves of rising tension, release and further tension. The visual style is one of the privileged point of view (often enhanced by the tracking camera appearing to hunt his characters down).

This taxonomy reveals the first possible weakness in auteur theory. The characteristics in this list are clearly those of the thriller genre. Is Hitchcock simply a (very good) thriller director? There are personal touches in Hitchcock's work: the ice-cold blonde leading lady, e.g. Tippi Hedren, Eve Marie Saint, Kim Novak or Grace Kelly; the black humour; the use of the 'macguffin' (a largely irrelevant detail which helps to drive the story on); and the great man's personal cameos (usually as a passer-by early in the film). None the less, the criticism does leave nagging doubts.

Perhaps the auteurist would be on safer ground with a director who worked in many genres, e.g. Godard's favourite candidate, Howard Hawks. Hawks certainly has his themes: action, professionalism under fire. His characters do show certain traits particularly linked to the air of understated professionalism about the world of much of Hawks' *œuvre*. In addition the female leads in many of Hawks' movies show an unusually strong sense of independence, e.g. Marie (Lauren Bacall) in *To Have and Have Not* (1944) or Feathers (Angie Dickinson) in *Rio Bravo* (1959).

There is no discernible 'Hawksian' narrative structure, not least because he worked with a vast range of material supplied by the studio from the widest possible range of sources. There are also major questions about identifying a Hawks visual style (beyond an ability to suit his style to the genre and a flair for an empowering framing of his leading characters).

Orson Welles – leading man, director, writer, etc. etc. on *Citizen Kane* – might seem a prime candidate. Yet even the seemingly invulnerable Welles has had his detractors. The critic Pauline Kael in *The Citizen Kane Book* (1972) points to the importance of Toland as cinematographer and Mankewizc as scriptwriter to the towering achievement. Welles' career after *Citizen Kane* – including losing control of *The Magnificent Ambersons* (1942) – illustrates that no film-maker can take on the role of lone creative genius.

Any attempt at a purist auteurism is undermined by even the most cursory knowledge of how film-making and the film industry operate. It could be argued that to 'qualify' as an auteur the director would have to do everything before, during and after the production of the film but it is better to see the 'auteur' as the orchestrator of a complex creative process – as portrayed in V. F. Perkins' *Film as Film* (1972). This approach does not lead to a thoughtless abandonment of the *politiques des auteurs* (which would be as bad as a slavish acceptance). Even at worst auteur theory can be seen – e.g. by Peter Wollen in *Signs and Meanings in the Cinema* (1972) – as a construct, but a useful one.

There are also arguments that other figures, apart from or in combination with, the director should be seen as attaining auteur status. Richard Corliss in *The Hollywood Screenwriters* (1975) puts forward an auteurist view which, by identifying *the writer*, is at the same time a complete antithesis of the *politiques*. Godard himself, via later film essays, e.g. *Histoire(s) du Cinema*, has identified the power of the producer and, in particular, Irving Thalberg's role at MGM. Richard Taylor in *The Politics of Soviet Cinema* (1979), etc., has pointed to the authority of various heads of the Soviet film industry and ultimately Joseph Stalin himself.

If everyone involved in a film begins to achieve auteur status we are fast approaching a position of denying any authorship. This view is at least in part supported by structuralist theory. Thus Roland Barthes in *Language/Image/Text* (1976) could write memorably of the 'death of the author'. Less strident structuralist-auteurist positions (as put forward by the magazine *Movie* in the 1970s) saw the author as one of many 'structures' influencing the final form and content of the film. None the less, to leave aside the ideological apparatus until the next chapter, certain individuals –

including Welles – at certain times do appear to have a strong personal input into their movies. This may be due to the force of their personality. This view, enshrined in American auteur theory, was led by Andrew Sarris via *The American Cinema* (1968): 'the strong director imposes his own personality on a film'. For Sarris the director's strength is measured in terms of the barriers he has to overcome. The result is a pantheon or league table of great directors of big films. Bazin was keen to distance himself from such machismo. The *Cahiers* school remained wedded to the idea of creativity within a cinematic system.

The identification of individual artists has its own biographical possibilities. The biographical approach is an element of 'auteurism'. It really works best when the auteur him/herself achieves star status (see previous chapter). This star status can be created by appearances before the camera and through subsidiary forms (see previous chapter), e.g. by Charlie Chaplin or Clint Eastwood, or through distinctive and personal contributions to high-profile productions, e.g. Stanley Kubrick and Martin Scorsese.

The biography of the director is only one way contextually to ground a film. In some cases it is particularly useful. Charles Spencer Chaplin was born in London, England in 1889. He died on Christmas Day, 1977. Central to Chaplin's world-view was that he was raised in poverty. His father died early of alcoholism and his mother went insane. He began his performing career in the music hall at the age of five. He toured England and later the US with Karno's London Comedians. In a moment of felicity that could have come from one of his own films he was spotted by early film impresario Mack Sennett and joined Keystone film company.

Chaplin started appearing in films in 1914, soon devising the character of the 'little tramp' with trademark baggy trousers, hat, cane and carefully trimmed moustache. He had transferred the faintly absurd mixture of poverty and carefully preserved dignity from his own English background on to the big screen. Later that same year he began directing himself. He was a household name by 1915. In 1918 he signed the film industry's first million-dollar contract. So far, so much 'star biography'. But Chaplin's authorial position comes from his directing (as well as acting and producing) and how he developed a personal style.

In the period from *The Gold Rush* (1925) to *City Lights* (1931) Chaplin was at the height of his fame and popularity. His subject matter and themes persist in film and television (particularly comedy) today. The underdog (the little tramp) is always surrounded by enormous bullies, but always survives by way of his wit and humour. If his films no longer look visually fresh or original today it is because everyone has copied him (as well as Harold Lloyd and Buster Keaton). Chaplin's authorial voice emerged from the pure comedy of the earlier films and developed the confidence to play moments of sentimental tragedy. The tramp character disappeared as Chaplin made more overtly political films such as *Modern Times* (1936) and *The Great Dictator* (1940). These films contain moments of comic genius but they are very didactic. Chaplin's popularity began to wane and declined further when the public reacted badly to *Monsieur Verdoux* (1947) in which he played a murderer. Chaplin's star image, as well as the audience's expectation of his authorial voice, had been stretched too far.

None the less the public remained fascinated by his life – not least because of romances with much younger women. Chaplin had never renounced his 'Englishness' and thus never became an American citizen. In the hysterical anti-communist atmosphere of the 1950s his previously much praised anti-fascist stance led to suspicion. After attending the London premiere of *Limelight* (1952) his re-entry to the USA was blocked. He then lived in exile in Switzerland, but was eventually knighted in England and awarded a 'lifetime achievement' Oscar in 1971 – accompanied by scenes of sentiment that would have fitted into his silent movies.

To see the 'auteur' function – and to test the validity of 'auteur theory' as a critical tool we can look at the careers of two great American directors form different eras. For the purposes of this exercise we have chosen John Ford and Martin Scorsese.

JOHN FORD

John Ford was born in Maine, USA in 1895. His real name, betraying his Irish roots, was Sean Aloysius O'Fearna. He worked in many genres over a long career and he won six Oscars – including two that he won for his World War II documentary work – but he is best known for his Westerns, such as *She Wore a Yellow Ribbon* (1949), *The Searchers* (1956) and *The Man Who Shot Liberty Valance* (1962). *Stagecoach* (1939) is arguably the Western that made Westerns respectable.

John Ford followed Frank, his older brother, an actor, into the movie business. At the end of his career, when asked what brought him to Hollywood, he replied 'the train'. John began as Jack Ford an actor playing 'dopey' in *The Mysterious Rose* (1914). He played a small part as a Klansman in Griffith's controversial epic *The Birth of a Nation* (1915) (again billed as Jack Ford) and made his final bow as a thespian as Buck – the scrapper – in *The Scrapper* (1917).

He went on to direct – as Jack Ford until 1924 and then as John – almost 150 films, beginning in 1917 with 10 films, including *The Tornado*, *The Trail of Hate* and *The Scrapper*. The writing credits dried up after 1919 but his first films as John Ford (director) – *Hearts of Oak* (1924) and *The Iron Horse* (1924) – also saw him take the credit as producer. Ford's directing style was dictatorial (if benevolent): 'I tell the actors what I want and they give it to me, usually on the first take.' John Wayne called him 'coach'.

Ford's first golden age coincided with the maturing of the classical Hollywood style. *Stagecoach*, *Young Mr. Lincoln* and *Drums Along the Mohawk* were all released in 1939. In *Stagecoach* we see a pure example of Ford's themes, narrative structure and features as well as visual style.

Ford's themes are the necessity for action and a personal morality which must (if necessary) override social regulation. The Fordian hero carries the burden of particular character traits in particular situations. His men (always men) are often isolated from civilisation/society. The women – even though Wayne's love interest in *Stagecoach* (1939) is a prostitute – are sentimentalised figures to be protected.

Stagecoach's narrative structure and features are of a piece with the Classical Hollywood style (see Chapter 5). The reason for this was that Ford was working frequently within the studio system for Daryl Zanuck at Fox. None the less, like all of the best 'product', Ford's films do contain elements of originality. In the case of *Stagecoach* there is a marvellously rich group of characters beyond the central hero and his girl.

The Fordian *mise en scène* is the homestead and the great outdoors (in this case, as in many Ford movies, Monument Valley). The action unfolds in a combination of vast outdoor vistas and tight, even claustrophobic, interiors. These settings are given a steadiness and grandeur by the use of sharp, deep-focus photography and keeping the camera static. This, as with *Citizen Kane*, could be seen as the product of the craft of Gregg Toland. However, this photographic style is consistent through Ford's mature work with or without Toland. Much like the photography, the editing is tight and perfunctory. Many of Ford's collaborators have claimed that he edited 'in the camera'. Ford, who learnt his trade in silent cinema, lets his (carefully controlled) actors tell the story through their actions and expressions.

Ford followed *Stagecoach* with four more films for Zanuck/Fox. *The Grapes of Wrath* and *The Long Voyage Home* (both 1940), *How Green Was My Valley* and *Tobacco Road* were all released before the USA entered the War in 1941. Ford then went on to lead an active service filming unit and to direct the documentary film *The Battle of Midway* (1942).

In the post-war period Ford appears to have developed a rather less certain and more humane approach to personality. This has led some critics (e.g. David Thompson) to identify an over-development of Ford's undoubted sentimentality. Others, including Lindsay Anderson, see Ford reaching new heights as a director with films such as *My Darling Clementine* (1946).

The cavalry trilogy of *Fort Apache* (1948), *She Wore a Yellow Ribbon* (1949) and *Rio Grande* (1950) are masterpieces of the genre – but they are notably genre pieces. Quite obviously, with a director like Ford who made his name in a particular style of picture there is also the question of authorship within *genre*. The question of genre can be seen as one of a structure to allow creative development much like a sonata form for an instrumental composer or a sonnet form for a poet. These structures can aid as well as restrict creativity. The great artist is able both to conform to the demands of the genre whilst simultaneously transcending the limitations such a structure presents – as can be seen in such shining examples as Mozart or Shakespeare.

In 1956 Ford made his finest mature work, *The Searchers*. In this film is it possible to argue that Ford did transcend genre. The *mise en scène* is quintessentially Fordian, i.e. Monument Valley. The cinematography (by Winton C. Hoch) has the Ford steadiness and grandeur. The frontier community is attacked. A hero arrives to settle scores and lead the narrative to resolution. But there are dark shadows in this work. We never really discover 'what makes a man to wander'. Ethan (Wayne) is the 'hero', i.e. the agent through which the narrative is brought to a conclusion, but much of the narrative is caused by his appalling behaviour. By the final reel the audience knows this man is no simple 'scrapper' (Buck in *The Scrapper*) or 'The Ringo Kid' (*Stagecoach*). He is a ruthless, driven killer. In a remarkable finish Wayne plays out a Freudian fantasy before being visually excluded from the homestead. The shot of the door closing on Wayne's iconographic figure is one of the most memorable in all cinema history.

The Searchers was made for Merian C. Cooper at Warner Brothers. Ford always operated within a studio system. Even after the Paramount decision (1948) reshaped the system Ford was always a company man. Much of his finest work was produced within one or other of the film factories. Therefore, beyond the 'film as collaborative art' caveat, there is an institutional problem. Unlike the auteur/genre problem the institutional query is rather more difficult to argue against. Who could be an 'auteur' in Hollywood anyway? One answer would be the producer. Rather more accurately we could consider the studio itself – possibly as personified by the studio head.

The story of the making of *Gone With The Wind* (see Chapter 5) gives us a candidate: David O. Selznick. David Selznick was born in 1902. The 'O' was invented later. He began his career working in Pittsburg for his father's newsreel company. He went on to set up his own independent newsreel company in New York. In 1924 Selznick produced his first feature film – Sam Taylor's *Roulette* – and headed for Hollywood and MGM (initially as a story editor). He was fired in 1927 and joined Paramount. There he produced, amongst other projects, *Four Feathers* (Cooper, 1929) and several William Wellman features. In 1930 Selznick married Irene Mayer and was hired as boss of RKO. There he produced many of George Cukor's movies before moving back to MGM in 1933, taking Cukor with him. In 1935 he formed his own company: Selznick International. His whole career appeared to lead to *Gone with the Wind*. Selznick hired lots of writers and overrode them. He hired three directors (Cukor, Wood, Fleming). His hand is definitely on the picture. Selznick was not the director but he bought the book, he developed the script, organised the shoot and hired (and fired) the talent. Selznick oversaw every shot. Here we have prima facie evidence of the producer as product manager – but no one film can prove 'authorial style'.

Following the view of authorship as team work we should not underestimate the influence of Selznick's brother Myron. According to the legend, in the light of the flames of the Atlanta set, Myron introduced David to his new client Vivien Leigh. Leigh was cast as Scarlett O'Hara on the spot.

Myron Selznick was David's older brother. Myron invented the concept of the agent for actors, directors and writers – even if they were under contract (as they were) he worked hard on their contracts. In the 1930s he represented William Wellman and George Cukor as well as Paulette Goddard, Charles Laughton and W. C. Fields, Laurence Olivier, Vivien Leigh and Alfred Hitchcock (once his brother had 'poached' the English auteur from Britain). The Selznicks presided over a part of the Hollywood of the 1930s and early 1940s. Myron was dead by 1944. David never reached the heights of *Gone With the Wind* again. The Selznicks constitute an extreme example – but then positioning the director as sole author is an extremely purist view too.

It is not fatuous to discuss the validity of viewing the producer as auteur. However, the grandiloquent personalities of David O. Selznick and – as another rare example – Howard Hughes are major exceptions. The most grandiose of the movie moguls did not interfere on a day-to-day basis with the actual film-making (although in the Golden Age of Hollywood their response to the dailies was absolutely crucial). The Hollywood moguls were fine packagers of talent and product. They were not in the business (or indeed in business) to visualise their themes and beliefs about character development. They are men of vision – but one of the visions was to help people make movies. In general 'the producer works to allow the auteur to create' (Joel Silver, *Empire* 10/2000).

Since 1948 and the Paramount decision (see Chapter 5), the role of the studio has been one of conduit for rather than instigator of talent. It has also been in the post-Paramount period that American auteur theory – e.g. Andrew Sarris (see above) has been developed and popularised. As the studio system transformed itself so the great American post-war auteur – Martin Scorsese – first entered a cinema.

MARTIN SCORSESE

Martin Scorsese is arguably *the* great American auteur and certainly one of the most important figures in contemporary cinema. He is responsible for films consistently voted 'best' of the decade: *Taxi Driver* (1976), *Raging Bull* (1980) and *Goodfellas* (1990). He is the director of more than 20 feature films – *from Who's that Knocking at My Door* (1968) through to *The Gangs of New York*. Many of these admittedly 'art-house' movies have gone on to make a discernible impact on popular culture around the world.

Scorsese is that rare thing: an American film director willing to take on the mantle of 'auteur'. Scorsese has placed himself within a European tradition of 'art' cinema whilst working within the institutional constraints of the American industry. A life-long movie lover, Scorsese's determination to become a film-maker only took hold when he failed to adapt to the rigours of training for his first chosen profession: the priesthood. The only alternative in his neighbourhood was crime; a career unsuited to a rather sickly boy. In a very real sense Scorsese is the priest of American cinema: keeping alive the flame through his work as campaigner, educator and archivist as well as director.

Scorsese is a very personal film-maker. Much of his work is centred on his religious/philosophical background and concerns. Many of the films are based in his Italian-American milieu. Scorsese has used his parents, Charles and Catherine Scorsese, in many of his movies. He 'appears' in some of his own films, most recently in *Bringing Out the Dead* (1999) supplying the voice of the dispatcher. In the 1970s the regularity of his appearances became almost Hitchcockian, e.g. as a brothel client in *Boxcar Bertha* (1972) and as Jimmy Shorts in *Mean Streets* (1973). In *Taxi Driver* (1976) Scorsese gives himself a major soliloquy as the psychotic passenger who observes his wife's silhouette from the back of Travis Bickle's cab. His films are also imbued with and enriched by his love for earlier movies. In *Mean Streets* the audience joins the central characters as they watch movies. The final shot of *Goodfellas* is of Joe Pesci recreating the final shot of Edwin S. Porter's *The Great Train Robbery*. In *Who's That Knocking at My Door* Harvey Keitel reminisces about Ford's *The Searchers*. *Taxi Driver* is on one level Scorsese's take on that classic movie. Both films present us with heroes back from a war; both heroes are isolated loners who find it difficult/impossible to adjust to or belong in the civilised world around them; both are trying to save a girl who does not want to be saved.

Scorsese has also portrayed himself as a 'director' in *The King of Comedy* (1983). In *After Hours* (1985) he operates the searchlight at Club Berlin and in *The Age of Innocence* (1993) he is the photographer. In *The Color of Money* (1986) he supplies the opening voice-over.

Although these personal appearances give his films a unique quality in themselves, Scorsese is best known – and achieves auteur status – through his direction. He graduated from New York University in 1964. In the 1960s he made interesting movies, including *It's Not Just You, Murray!* (1964) and *Who's That Knocking at My Door?* (1968) as well as acting as assistant director on *Woodstock* (1970), editing *Woodstock* as well as *Elvis On Tour* (1972).

Producer Roger Corman offered Scorsese the chance to direct a feature with a budget (however tiny) with *Boxcar Bertha* (1972). What followed was two decades of outstanding creativity, a series of truly great films which gave Martin Scorsese his 'auteur as star' image. Scorsese hit his personal creative stride with three master-pieces: *Mean Streets*, *Alice Doesn't Live Here Anymore* and *Taxi Driver*. These films and the ones that followed are identifiable as Scorsesean through their visual style, narrative structure and features, particular character traits/situations and sets of themes.

Scorsese is the quintessentially cinematic auteur. His films – whatever material they are based upon – could only be presented as films. This 'film-ness' is a direct result of his complete immer-sion in the history of cinema. His understanding of the tradition has led him to work with outstanding film craftsmen (Boris Leven, Saul Bass, Freddie Francis, *et al.*) and composers with long associ-ations with film (from Bernard Hermann to Philip Glass). In addi-tion Scorsese has been attracted to remake and sequel projects which allowed him to become part of the Hollywood tradition he so admires, e.g. *The Color of Money* and *Cape Fear* (1991).

There is no denying that Scorsese has always exhibited, indeed revelled in, the use of technique and cutting edge technology. As such he is in the tradition of Orson Welles. As with Welles this desire is absolutely linked to a desire to tell powerful stories in as direct and engaging a way as possible. Scorsese avoided being submerged in the niceties of production design in *The Age of Innocence*, narrative complexity in *Casino* (1995) or by technical fireworks (especially in the editing) in *Bringing out the Dead*. His films succeed in telling powerful stories above all because of a firm footing in character.

Scorsese's visual style is 'nervous' – and thus at one with the character types and narratives he has usually focused on. The camera is mobile. It – and thus the viewers' point of view – is constantly tracking and panning. Our perceptions are both height-ened and disorientated by zooming through different planes of the action. Scorsese has made the 'zoom in dolly out' trick his own (e.g. in the chilling coffee bar scene between De Niro and Liotta towards the denouement of *Goodfellas*). Cinematic brio is under-lined and accentuated by a vast array of editing techniques which enervate the visuals and cause the viewer to doubt their own perceptions. Scorsese's visual élan is of course a product of collaboration with very talented cinematographers – especially Michael Chapman and, since 1980, editor Thelma Schoonmaker.

Scorsese's trademark narrative structure and features – the use of voice-over, hallucinogenic disjunctures and jarring changes of pace are also a result of collaboration, e.g. with Paul Schrader on both *Taxi Driver* and *Bringing out the Dead*. The narrative similarity between these films is not coincidental. None the less Scorsese does work on the screenplay and has served as a writer of his own films, e.g. *The Gangs of New York*, beginning with *What's a Nice Girl Like You Doing in a Place Like This?* (1963), *It's Not Just You, Murray!* (1964) and *Who's That Knocking at My Door?* (1968), and including several of his most important features from *Mean Streets* through parts of *The Last Temptation of Christ* (1988) and much of *Goodfellas*.

Through the student shorts, the 1970s classics, the problematic *New York, New York* and *Raging Bull* and *The King of Comedy* (all milestones in their own right) and into the mature works of the last dozen years, Scorsese has continued to reflect upon the great themes of human existence. Often his personal and intelligent stance has appeared at odds with the spirit of the times, even in a genre piece like the remake of *Cape Fear* (1991).

Scorsese's films are essentially character-driven. As he commented on *Mean Streets*: 'The plot wasn't anything. It was the characters that mattered.' His characters are marginalised loners struggling with inner demons. This state of mind suits his cinematic style and vice versa. Usually the central character is male. These male characters invariably struggle with what masculinity does (or is supposed to) mean within the social or familial codes that dominate them. Obvious examples of these 'Scorsese men' are Travis Bickle (*Taxi Driver*) and Jake La Motta (*Raging Bull*). Both parts were played by Robert De Niro. De Niro's performance was no less charged with pent-up frustration and hardly less menacing in – ostensibly – a musical *New York, New York* (1977). Both predator and prey, Max Cady (De Niro) and Sam Bowden (Nick Nolte), in *Cape Fear* are driven by inner demons and neurosis.

These classic 'Scorsese men' invariably fail to come to terms with personal and social pressures. Their frustrations inevitably result in explosions of violence. More recent developments in the director's exploration of this issue can be sourced from the turning point of *The Color of Money* (where Paul Newman portrays a new type of older, more ambiguous 'Scorsese man') and *The Last Temptation of Christ* through *The Age of Innocence* to *Kundun* (1998) and *Bringing out the Dead*. In each of these films the male protagonist internalises his conflicts and works them through more or less constructively (whilst remaining consistent to personal honour).

The centrality of men in Scorsese's films has tended to draw attention away from his representation of women which goes beyond the more obvious woman as Madonna/whore (e.g. in *Who's That Knocking at My Door*, *Mean Streets*, *Taxi Driver*) Scorsese's films have presented us with a number of strong female characters who have sought to undermine the roles imposed upon them by men, e.g. Alice (*Alice Doesn't Live Here Anymore*) and Ellen (*The Age of Innocence*) as well as Paulette in 'Life Lessons' (*New York Stories*) and even Ginger (*Casino*). The fact that these women – like Scorsese's men – also appear cursed to failure is a further area of interest in his work.

Scorsese's thematic obsessions are the stuff of life: love, sex, death and duty. Scorsese has worked through these themes over a period of 30 years. His themes are of personal and public pressure. Guilt and redemption (undoubtedly springing from a powerful Catholicism) recur throughout his work as does an unglamorised confrontation with unrelenting cathartic violence, e.g. in *Mean Streets*, *Taxi Driver*, *Raging Bull*, *Goodfellas* and *Casino*.

The films which do not fit the urban crime (one is tempted to say Scorsesean) sub-genre, e.g. *The King of Comedy*, are still driven by the Scorsesean themes of the loner, overpowering psychological drives and extremes of behaviour. Even the comedy has a dark, uncontrolled, violent side. In films as diverse in subject matter as *The Last Temptation of Christ*, *The Age of Innocence* and *Casino* we are presented with variations on Scorsese's concerns observed in his own way and with the bravura film-making we have come to expect from 'A Martin Scorsese film'.

A film-maker can only claim (or be offered) auteur status if we can identify characteristics of subject matter and visual style. Auteurs must be seen to present their world view. The next chapter attempts to come to terms with how the world views of movies are presented, received and utilised.

10 The medium and the message

Representation, audience and spectatorship

> I don't think I'm going to let you stay in the film business.
> (Chas (Edward Fox) in *Performance* (Roeg, 1968))

Representation – the way of showing – is a social process (i.e. it requires the interaction of several people) through which signs (including moving images) are made to convey meaning. Because the representation of anything involves organisation and selection, it has ideological potential.

A key area for students of film is the way film represents various cultures, subcultures and identities. A medium as powerful as cinema needs to be interrogated as to the messages and values carried. As a case-study this chapter will look at these issues centring on the representation of class (particularly the importance of social class in determining characters' behaviour) and gender (particularly in terms of change and continuity) in British crime movies of the post-war period. This approach will also allow us to decide if films construct a representation of national identity. After all – apart from the heritage/empire films that have dulled the senses of so many audiences – the caper movie is *the* British genre.

THE BLUE LAMP (1950)

The Blue Lamp was directed by Basil Dearden from a script by T. E. B. Clarke. Clarke, an ex-policeman, was, like Dearden, a stalwart of the Ealing Studio, having scripted amongst others *Hue and*

The iconic Brit gangster – a text for consumption or subversion, *Get Carter* (2000). Reproduced with permision from BFI Stills, Posters and Designs

Cry (Crichton, 1947) and *Passport to Pimlico* (Cornelius, 1949). After *The Blue Lamp* he worked on *The Lavender Hill Mob* (Crichton, 1951).

The film is a fascinating document for the historian of film and possibly the student of social attitudes (at least amongst middle-class film-makers). It is less useful for anyone looking for social reality; e.g. the film is of a piece with the regular moral panics about violent crime. The opening narration states that Britain is in the grips of a 'crime wave'. However, statistics show that the crime rate fell in the late 1940s.

The film follows the daily routine and domestic quietism of two London policemen: the veteran George Dixon (Jack Warner) and the rookie Andy Mitchell (Jimmy Hanley). Meanwhile two young, feckless men – Tom Riley (played by a drippingly beautiful Dirk Bogarde) and Spud (Patric Doonan) – have turned to crime. They plan a series of robberies with Tom's girl Diana (Peggy Evans) – a sulky and discontented beauty – as 'insider'.

As *The Blue Lamp* is a movie, representation – and the ideological apparatus behind it – is a matter of how characters are filmed as well as what they do and say. The class representation in *The Blue Lamp* is interesting because almost all of the characters are 'working class'. The rare exceptions are a caricatured drunken 'toff' (Cameron Hall) and – rather more significantly – the detectives who are clearly marked out by accent as a class above their men.

The Blue Lamp is set in a working-class milieu, but this is a stratified working class. PC Dixon's household is classic working-class aristocracy – not rich but 'comfortable' and a cut above Diana's tenement block seen early in the film. Dixon, his family and friends sit around the kitchen table with an easy familiarity discussing manure. This agricultural discussion allows us to see them as prosperous and proud of their 'land' (albeit an allotment). Mrs Dixon (Gladys Henson) feigns a shocked reaction that displays a middle-class nicety.

Beyond the script, the *mise en scène* hammers home social messages. External shots of the Dixon home (e.g. as the news of Dixon's death arrives) show a pleasant, wide street full of politely playing, neatly dressed children. This sense of order is graphically compared to the environs of the 'lumpenproletariat' that are messy in and outdoors.

The importance of social class in determining characters' behaviour is presented – in a profoundly unsubtle manner – when these social milieux are presented in juxtaposition; e.g. as when a scene in which we see Tom's derelict living conditions follows a scene of the Dixon's domestic bliss.

The different strata of the working class are identified by their personal relationships. Early in the film the police are called to Diana's home to deal with domestic violence. It is rather chilling to see that in 1950 such a case could be treated as a joke. There is an air of violence about the young criminals too. The first on-screen meeting of the gang portrays them as surly and awkward:

Diana Lewis: What d'ya think I am? Soft or something?
Spud: Yeah.

This brief dialogue highlights questions of gender relations in *The Blue Lamp*. The men in George Dixon's household would not dream of talking to 'Ma' in the rude manner of Spud. The female role is subordinate but has its own strengths. Honest frugality and standards are upheld (or in the case of Diana not upheld) by the woman.

The 'gang' have no such moral centre. In their second crime – the hold-up of a cinema – Dixon is shot. This crime is beyond the pale even for career (i.e. 'decent') criminals. Eventually and inevitably Tom gets caught. He has not followed the 'code' of the 'professional' thief. At the end of the film the criminal 'boss' helps the police to apprehend Tom at the racetrack.

The film is pro-establishment and very much in defence of the status quo (even criminals should know their place). It set out to give a moral message to the youth of post-war Britain. Tom's arrest punches home the simple message of this most straightforward of films: crime does not pay. Within a decade British films were taking a much more ambivalent approach to authority and casting doubt on the moral certainties as portrayed in the 1950s.

PERFORMANCE (1968)

Performance – the quintessential counter-culture film, directed by Donald Cammel and Nic Roeg – was finally released, in a studio re-edited version, in 1970. Warner Brothers were still wary of their strange child but calculated that sex, drugs and Mick Jagger were worth some ticket sales. Thus the film was sold: 'See them all in a film about fantasy. And reality. Vice. And versa.'

Chas (James Fox), a psychotic gangster, needs a place to lie low after going way beyond his boss Harry Flowers' orders. ('He likes his work' … 'that's the half of it'.) He finds cover in a Notting Hill mansion owned by Turner (Jagger), a reclusive rock superstar. As Chas – posing as a 'juggler' – puts it: 'I need a bohemian atmosphere!'

Roeg and Cammell created a visually complex and disturbing juxtaposition between two subcultures with their own twisted sense of glamour. Turner, initially repulsed, becomes intrigued by Chas's air of violence and directness. (Turner: 'that carpet is over a thousand years old'. Chas: 'Yeh . . . looks like it.') As the title suggests the film is all about performances. As Turner puts it to Chas: 'The only performance that makes it, that makes it all the way, is the one that achieves madness. Am I right? Eh?'

Chas – initially scornful of the bohemians ('weirdos . . . free love') is drawn into Turner's underground world. He becomes

Vice and versa, *Performance* (1968). Reproduced with permission from BFI Stills, Posters and Designs

interested in Turner's lover Pherber (Anita Pallenberg), and her 'friend' Lucy (Michèle Breton). When he is given magic mushrooms his sense of certainty starts to unravel as he finds his sexuality being brought into question.

Roeg and Cammell's representation of gender goes from a parody of aggressive maleness (brief glimpses of male dominant 'S & M' during the credits sequence), through an exploration of the homoerotic potential of violence (Chas and his nemesis Joey Maddocks). Finally, as identities blend in Turner's world so does sexual identity; e.g. Pherber holds up a mirror to Chas to reflect her female image onto him.

Performance's representation of class is full of strange detail. The criminals are obviously (London) working class by accent but they are strange proletarians. They have a sense of poise – even languidity – missing in the frenetic behaviour of the criminals in *The Blue Lamp*. They exhibit a strange choice of reading matter, e.g. Borges (Rosebloom in the car) or gay pornography (Harry Flowers in bed).

The film is packed with disorientation; e.g. Turner becomes a singing 'Harry Flowers' in the 'Memo from Turner' sequence – who is 'the man who squats behind the man who works the soft machine?' (a reference to William Burroughs' description of the human race). At the end of this most fragmentary of films Turner and Chas appear to switch identities – although Chas has already apparently murdered Turner.

Performance is very much a part of the late 1960s–early 1970s. Its politics and therefore its representational style are about individual identity. By the 1990s – with the fall of European Communism and the seeming lack of ideological differences between major political movements – politics itself appeared to have become an irrelevance. None the less, the apolitical stance is in itself a politically charged position – and requires its own representations.

LOCK STOCK AND TWO SMOKING BARRELS (1998)

Guy Ritchie's (successful) attempt to relaunch the grand British tradition of the caper movie has spawned a host of poor copies (including his own *Snatch* (2000)). The film was successfully marketed with a jokey lack of concern for its subject matter: 'They lost half a million at cards but they've still got a few tricks up their sleeve' and – in an unwitting reference to the plot of *The Blue Lamp* – 'A Disgrace to Criminals Everywhere'.

The film is a well-made piece of entertainment. It is funny and fast-paced, so fast that the audience does not get the time to ask whether we should be laughing. The story line is convoluted and very silly, but strength of plot is hardly the point of this entertainment.

'*Lock, Stock . . .*' is the story of four 'lads'. It is a very male film. The representation of gender relations is hardly an issue. There is no relationship. Although a discussion of the absence of women – and why – could prove fruitful (see the discussion of 'theory' later in this chapter). One of the comic elements in the film is the strange tenderness of the relationship between a brutal enforcer Big Chris (Vinnie Jones) and his son 'Little Chris' (Peter McNicholl), angelic of face but wise beyond his years.

> Little Chris: 'Fuckin' hell John, do you always walk around with this in your pocket?'
> Big Chris: 'Hey! You use language like that again son, you'll wish you hadn't!'

As Big Chris leaves the lads empty handed: All right, son: roll them guns up, count the money, and put your seat belt on.

The film does have some points to make about masculinity. Ostensibly the message appears to be that being a 'good bloke' can be reduced to a stance of 'having a laugh' under any and all circumstances.

Plank: Ah! They shot me!
Dog: Well, shoot 'em back!

The gang consists of a new 'Tom' (Jason Flemyng) and Eddie (Nick Moran) with Soap (Dexter Fletcher) and Bacon (Jason Statham) instead of Spud. This motley crew are more in the tradition of Bogarde and Doonan than Fox and his 'organisation'. They find themselves heavily in debt to gang boss 'Hatchet' Harry Lonsdale after losing half a million pounds in a card game. They overhear their neighbours plotting to hold up a group of drug growers. The lads decide to stitch up the robbers in turn. Confusion is added to this basic caper scenario by the theft of a pair of antique shotguns (which 'Hatchet' wants). Of course their master plan goes seriously wrong. Tom: 'There's no money; there's no weed. It's all been replaced by a pile of corpses.' These young criminals are dodgy lads rather than evil and manipulative gangsters. Even the real 'heavies' – like 'Rory Breaker' have a comic turn of phrase: 'If the milk turns out to be sour, I ain't the kinda pussy to drink it.' Or – most memorably: 'If you hold back anything, I'll kill ya. If you bend the truth or I think you're bending the truth, I'll kill ya. If you forget anything I'll kill ya. In fact, you're gonna have to work very hard to stay alive, Nick. Now do you understand everything I've said? Because if you don't, I'll kill ya.'

The cinematography works to engage us in the lads' plight, e.g. their actions are usually matched in motion by the camera. We are positioned 'in' the gang rather than as the dispassionate observer.

Other characters, e.g. the debt-collector, some public school 'chemists', the psychotic drugs dealer, are all caricatures we might expect to see in a comedy. The public school-boys are examples of particularly reductionist class representation. The lack of class conflict and/or interaction is to some extent substituted by the tensions of the north–south divide. Lenny: 'I hate these southern fairies!'

The representation of the working class is simple too. To be working class is to be funny (and/or not very bright) thus the film is driven by sharp one-liners or seriously dumb dialogue; e.g. Tom: 'It's kosher as Christmas.' Nick the Greek: 'The Jews don't celebrate Christmas, Tom.'

After a good deal of gun (and knife) play the plot reaches a bizarre (very funny), unresolved ending literally 'hanging' from a bridge. As such the film tunes in with the grand tradition of British (comic) caper movie, the best of which is *The Italian Job* (Collinson, UK, 1969)

The most famous – and quoted – line in the film is Big Chris's parting shot to the lads: 'It's been emotional.' The joke is that of course 'it' – and the film – has not been.

Does Ritchie have a 'preferred reading'? What does he want us to see and think whilst watching his movie? Does he care? – is it that important in so amoral a world where our sympathy goes to whichever of the (moronic) criminals has the funnier lines.

Study of representation focuses on what is presented and how i.e. what the film-makers wants us to see (the 'preferred reading'). The concept of 'preferred reading' was popularised by the Centre for Cultural Studies at Birmingham (UK) following Stuart Hall's 1983 article, 'The determination of news photographs'. Hall discussed the techniques employed to 'close off the reader' from independent interpretations. This view was at least in part influenced by Umberto Eco's *The Role of the Reader* (1981), which claimed that texts can be open or closed (which is true – but more or less, rather than absolutely) and that popular culture texts were largely closed (which – as we shall see – is wrong). This approach to mass media (including film) accepts the buying power without reckoning on the imaginative power of all of us – the audience – or 'Those wonderful people in the dark' as Norma Desmond (played by Gloria Swanson) so memorably dubbed us all in *Sunset Boulevard* (Wilder, USA, 1950).

Much recent film and media theory centres itself on the viewer. So our focus for analysis moves from 'what is on the screen (and why)' – to 'what do we *do* with the material presented' either as a group (the audience) or as an individual (the spectator).

Film – particularly when viewed on a big screen in the dark – is a powerfully mediated and *moving* medium; none the less the belief in a 'hypodermic syringe' (the idea that people will simply copy things they've seen in the media) is no longer a tenable position. To quote an influential theorist, David Gauntlett: 'The whole problem with the media effects research is that it takes place in that depressing corner of "communications" research which places more value on a veneer of "scientific" method than it does on actually saying anything.' Gauntlett's book *Moving Experiences* (1995) works hard to expose much of this pseudo-science.

Much current academic work on audiences focuses on precisely how the audience *uses* media texts, thus abandoning the approach of earlier theorists like McQuail (*Towards a Sociology of Mass Communications*, 1969) who amongst seven more or less true characteristics included the fallacy that audiences are 'united by a common focus of interest'. Just because they are all looking in the same direction does *not* mean they are all seeing the same thing.

The cartoonish oversimplified view of the homogenous audience 'acted upon' by the 'closed text' produced by insidious monopoly capitalists is a hangover from the views of the Frankfurt School, e.g. Adorno and Marcuse. Adherents to the Frankfurt school will remain deeply worried by mass culture (where subjectivity would become 'a mere object of exchange-value'. They may see the modern consumer (as Adorno in *The Culture Industry*, Marcuse and Walter Benjamin did) as vulnerable, fragmented, passive and thus easily influenced.

Later media sociologists (e.g. Ang in *Desperately Seeking the Audience* (1999) and Morley in *Television* (1992)) have abandoned grand theory and tended towards the study of groups of individuals to see how they actually consume popular culture. This focus on social context and the relationship between text/groups has a basis in the wide range of empirical work done by social anthropologists (e.g. Dick Hebdidge, *Subcultures* (1972)). The sociologists and anthropologists in their own way hit upon the same idea as the post-structuralist and postmodernist theorists: polysemy. Media texts could and would be read in different ways by different groups.

It would be difficult to defend a position that claimed the movies are utterly lacking in power to influence. The issue becomes whether that influence is consistently effective or even consistent in nature (which it is not) or to what extent a single film or production of the movie industry can influence an audience at a particular time in a particular circumstance. More realistic and less hysterical than a 'hypodermic syringe' view would be that film – or a film – could be a medium for 'agenda setting'. Although it is worth pointing out that D. W. Griffith's attempt to set the anti-war agenda with *Intolerance* (1916) began a history of notable failure. Dictators from Stalin onwards have never failed to be disappointed at the propaganda failure of 'the most important of all the arts'.

A claim to a lesser level of influence is that of 'reinforcement' – that media texts can act by underpinning or normalising ways of seeing and behaving. This more persuasive and realistic view was popularised by Lazarsfeld *et al.* when discussing the role of the press influencing political debate and preferences in *The People's Choice* (1948).

Vastly experienced distributors and exhibitors are all too often caught out by the actions of the audience at local, regional, or international level. Hollywood studios spend vast amounts of time and money on surveys and focus groups, trying to guess what its audience will consume, never mind how they will consume it. The minefield that is attempting to make generalisations about an audience can only become even trickier when dealing with individual spectators.

The viewer's sense of identification with what occurs on screen is central to the film-going experience. There is a great potential for pleasure in merging another, more glamorous identity with one's own. In Lacanian analysis, e.g. in *Ecrits* (1966, English translation published 1977), the film's diegesis could be considered a perfect idealised world (with a potential to live out our wildest desires). Some of cinema's attraction lies in the power of the 'point of view' (POV) shot. POV not only ties the viewer to the (usually) central character whose view-point we share, but also by its nature gives that view a privileged position. The use of flashback – in essence a prolonged POV – can underline this privileged view.

Theories of spectatorship began to take hold in film studies with the popularisation of psychoanalytical frameworks and especially the work of Christian Metz (e.g. *Essays on the Significance of Cinema* (1971 and 1972) – translated as *Film Language* (1974)) and others including Baudry and Bellour. These theorists took a Freudian view of the (male) spectator sitting in the dark re-enacting an Oedipal trajectory. The spectator was simply a voyeur drawn into the film world. Before long this position was challenged by Laura Mulvey (in 'Visual pleasure and narrative cinema' *Screen* 3, 1975). She further defined Metz's view of spectatorship into 'scopophilia' (pleasure in viewing). Following on from Freud, Mulvey saw this pleasure developing from a (male) desire to dominate and punish the female object.

This view of cinema as being centred on 'the male gaze' rather left women in the picture but out of the audience. Do they simply assume the male position (thus allowing them to experience power) or do they actually identify with and enjoy the passivity? Much theoretical readings of film since Mulvey's polemic – including her own work – has centred on trying to either figure this out or refute such a potentially disturbing reading of the film experience. Whatever the view taken, the relationship between spectator and screen has increasingly been seen as complex and far from unitary.

Popular mainstream films are often accused of reinforcing dominant values and lulling audiences into a passive acceptance, not least of the dominant 'male gaze'. Yet the whole process of consumption has the potential to complicate any medium, never mind one so full of potentialities as film. In other words 'it is all a bit more complicated than that'. As solid a vehicle as the most staid of British crime thrillers can be open to readings way beyond the intentions of the Ealing Studio. In the words of respected cultural commentator Andy Medhurst on *The Blue Lamp*: 'Bogarde is "erotic and compelling" while his counterpart Jimmy Hanley (PC Andy Mitchell) playing the rookie policeman is "bland and neutered".'

If fare this plain is open to such interpretation, then material as deliberately rich as thrillers by such playful masters as Alfred Hitchcock (e.g. in *Vertigo* (1958); *Marnie* (1962)) or the more baroque creations of Brian de Palma (e.g. *Dressed to Kill* (1980)) are surely fields of unlimited self-expression and fulfilment.

Theoretical positions have tried desperately to keep up with the audience and spectator (as well as changes in the content and production practices of film and other media). Structuralism, fuelled by the semiology of Saussure, the philosophy of Barthes as well as the psychology of Lacan, sought out deep unconscious assumptions and structures. The 1960s structuralist 'rethinking' of film theory – including a concerted attempt to crush auteur theory – should be seen (as noted by Hayward in *Cinema Studies: The Key Concepts* (2000) as (a) an ideological construct itself and (b) an attempt to import theory from other fields – most of which (apart from the interesting if less than easily explained case of Lacanian psychoanalytical theory) provided more heat than light.

Post-structuralism at least had the benefit of asking us to question pre-eminent claims to truth. This questioning approach also offered the powerful refusal to accept a single grand narrative or overarching theory. The intimately linked conceptual approach generically labelled 'postmodernism' brought with it an important questioning of the relationship between author and text and between text and consumer. Postmodernism – via the work of Jacques Derrida, e.g. *Of Grammatology* (1976) and *Writing and Difference* (1978) – deconstructed even the solid existence of a 'text'. The concept of 'difference' proposes that all writing (including in light) is impure and all descriptions entail an unbridgeable gap. Gaps and dualities between reality, intent, representation and reception are central to Lacan's idea of 'playfulness' (*jouissance*). If the idea of a single text deliberately given a readily understood meaning was under threat what chance could there be for a simple text–consumer relationship? Lyotard in *The Post Modern Condition* (1984) posited the subject as acting on, as well as acted upon, by the text. Identity and identity construction become central to investigation of cultural consumption.

Any contemporary discussion of identity has to take note of the work and influence of Michel Foucault. Foucault challenged the 'common sense' view of people that they have a single self-contained identity or character. For Foucault the 'real' identity does not exist. Identity is communicated to others by interactions. It is a shifting construction.

Foucault's lifelong interest was in power relations. For Foucault, power cannot be possessed, only exercised. Where there is power (even as hegemonic as Hollywood!) there is potentially resistance. Foucault's position has been taken up and extended by Judith Butler. She is currently the most well-known and persuasive theorist of power, gender, sexuality and identity. In her most influential book *Gender Trouble* (1990), Butler argued against (feminism's) regulation of gender relations reinforcing a binary view of gender relations in which human beings are divided into two clear-cut groups, women and men. Butler preferred to see the possibility for a person to form and choose their own individual identity. Gender should be seen as 'a relation among socially constituted subjects in specifiable contexts' (p. 12). In other words, rather than being a fixed attribute in a person, gender is a fluid variable that shifts and changes in different contexts and at different times.

Butler argues against the simplistic view that sex (male, female) is seen to cause gender (masculine, feminine) and desire. Butler, inspired in part by Foucault, attempted to break the links between these, so that gender and desire are flexible, free-floating and not 'caused' by other stable factors: 'There is no gender identity behind the expressions of gender . . . identity is performatively constituted by the very "expressions" that are said to be its results' (*Gender Trouble*, p. 25).

In other words – and the links to Roeg and Cammell's movie have been pointed out by Colin MacCabe (in the BFI Classic on *Performance*) amongst others – gender is a performance. This idea of identity as free-floating performance, is one of the key ideas in 'queer theory'.

Butler suggests that certain cultural configurations of gender have seized a hegemonic hold (i.e. they have come to seem natural in our culture). She recommends subversive action – 'gender trouble'. Gender trouble has obvious media – including film – implications. The mass media is the primary means for images – alternative or otherwise – to be disseminated. The media is therefore the site upon which this 'semiotic war' (a war of symbols, of how things are represented) would take place if anywhere – and you thought film was just entertainment!

Theory – particularly on identity – is a fast-moving and increasingly complex and fascinating area of discussion. This book can help to introduce the reader to the subject – mainly as a way of pointing out the further avenues that the study of film can take us to (and as a warning against any one methodology becoming dominant). No one book can give a reader all the information required for theoretical investigation. We would recommend http://www.theory.org.uk. This 'theory' site is the work of David Gauntlett. (Many thanks must go to Dr Gauntlett for helping the authors with their enquiries about theoretical constructs in communications.) Some readers will not wish to take the theoretical approach to film studies, or even to concentrate on the consumption as opposed to the production of film. They will prefer our own site: http://www.internationalfilm.org.

The key point to keep in mind is that theories and positions on film should only be followed if they are useful, i.e. gain the reader deeper insight and/or enjoyment of the moving image.

11 Bringing it all together

In this concluding chapter the authors present close textual and contextual readings of *Star Wars* (Lucas, USA, 1977). We have chosen *Star Wars*, the film voted best film of all time by the readers of *Empire* magazine in September 1999, to be our 'text' in order to attempt an analysis that draws on all the 'positions' discussed in this book because it is a phenomenally successful global cultural product. In the year of its release *Star Wars* became the biggest box-office hit of all time. On its re-release in 1997 (with the sound remixed and the addition of some digitised sections added) it took $46 million in its first week and became the first film to gross more than $400 million at the US box-office. The distributor's press book for the special edition (1997) proclaimed: 'While *Star Wars* was a defining event for one generation, it has been embraced by new generations assuring its place as a timeless epic of grand design and boundless fun.' This claim was confirmed by articles in *Time*, *Newsweek*, the *New Yorker* and the *New York Times*, which said that the film was 'part of the culture' and its 'lessons' about good and evil, humanity and technology, pride and redemption were a 'very powerful force indeed'. These publications commented that contemporary mass media are full of references to the film and that many words and phrases from them have entered into everyday life. The most striking example of this must surely be the appropriation of the film's title to describe Ronald Reagan's missile defence programme in the mid-1980s. In other words it is a film of enormous impact, both in terms of its effect on the film industry and on the American culture/sense of national identity. The film can also serve as the paradigm for mainstream film in the late twentieth century – crossing genres and revelling in spectacle – and the model for the technological and marketing revolution we are beginning to experience in the early twenty-first century.

MISE EN SCÈNE

Setting

The different sets created by Lucas (and his team: production designer John Barry, art directors Leslie Dilley and Norman Reynolds plus set decorators Roger Christian and Steve Cooper) are absolutely crucial to the final impact of *Star Wars*. The sets both establish the genre and create the impact of a film that depends for much of its effect on spectacle. What can be more spectacular than the realistic space settings and the gripping spectacle of the pursuit, escape and conflict central to the narrative of the film? A detailed look at the opening sequence establishes this. The film opens with an image of a black, star-filled galaxy into which the title and text appear rolling from the foreground to the background of the picture. As the words move into the background they become illegible, mere points of light like the surrounding stars. Thus the sense of a vast landscape is created through the exaggerated depth of field.

The audience is presented with a new landscape, a new canvas, a new frontier against which an old story is going to be played out. As the opening text proclaims this is a tale of good versus evil, of a runaway princess seeking freedom from tyranny. Here in these first few seconds of film the key to *Star Wars* is revealed. What Lucas has done is to take old familiar stories, a *bricolage* of the fairytale, the Western, the samurai epic and add the twist of novelty and spectacle by relocating the action to his fabulous and fantastic space sets.

Once the narrative context has been established by the opening text the camera tilts down to reveal in closer proximity a planet, a moon and a sun and against this backdrop the first space chase takes place. Princess Leia's rebel spaceship flies into the foreground of the frame. Slowly it becomes smaller and more distant as it disappears into the background, following the same path as the preceding text. It is followed first by the nose and then the massive, seemingly never-ending body of the Empire's ship, engaged upon capture. Now the impact of the exaggerated depth of field described above is fully felt, as by emphasising the vastness of the Empire's spaceship it suggests the vastness of the Empire's power and, by contrast, the vulnerability of the rebels. In this one image impossible odds for our small band of heroes are created and so the excitement of a David and Goliath conflict begins. The three-dimensional effect of this shot and the verisimilitude with which the spaceships are presented make this a truly spectacular opening. It has been copied many times since but in 1977 it was the first time audiences were treated to images of ships gliding through space without seeing the models wobble and betray their cardboard origins.

The shots described above are elaborate, even fantastic, opening shots that function to seize our attention and kick-start the narrative by plunging us straight into an on-going story-line. In traditional continuity style they also function as establishing shots, establishing, with the aid of the accompanying text, where the action is taking place. Once the overall location has thus been made clear, the action cuts to an interior and we see the first of the spaceship sets. This is Princess Leia's beleaguered ship. We see the two 'droids', R2-D2 and C3PO fleeing down a long corridor that has a metallic pristine look to it and is dominated by the pure white colour of walls and floor and the white lights in the ceiling. Black, electronic-looking control panels are dotted about on the walls and by the doors, which are electronically sealed. The whole effect is of a high-tech antiseptic purity. We can compare this to the interior sets of the other spaceships used in the film – the *Millennium Falcon* and the *Death Star*. The *Millennium Falcon* lacks the pure, clean lines of colour and space seen in the princess's ship. It appears to be smaller, more ramshackle, less uniform in its design. The overall effect is of a ship that is rickety, idiosyncratic but trustworthy. Rather like its owner, Han Solo, the *Falcon* doesn't look too promising but comes through in the end: the set acts as a reflection of the character of its owner, a fact increased by the way in which Han anthropomorphises and defends his ship.

This use of the set as a means of creating, or at least reinforcing character is true elsewhere in the film. If we look back at the pure, pristine whiteness of the princess's ship we can read this use of colour symbolically. Leia's character is pure and good, both qualities denoted by the use of the colour white. We can compare this with the interior sets of the *Death Star* where black, the symbolic colour of evil, is the dominant colour and vastness the primary theme. Like the *Millennium Falcon* and the princess's ship, the *Death Star* is an extension of the character of its owner, i.e. The Empire. It is huge, powerful, ominous and destructive. Its final miraculous destruction symbolises the triumph of good over evil.

Our first image of the interior of the *Death Star* presents us with its key figures apparently in conference. We see them seated around a huge table that dominates the room. In its shape the table might remind us of the Round Table of Arthurian legend but its black, reflective surface denotes something altogether darker in purpose and this is further suggested by the grey uniforms, iconographic of fascism, of those seated around the table. If Princess Leia in her white clothes and white ship symbolises a force for good then Darth Vader, all in black in this black room symbolises evil.

The planet set is where we meet the two heroes of the film, Luke Skywalker and Han Solo. The differences in these two characters are delineated through the different locations in which we find them. Luke, the youthful, innocent boy is isolated on his uncle's farm. Han, the more decadent and experienced man of the world, is found amongst the smugglers and thieves of the saloon that is appropriately described by Ben (Obi-wan) Kenobi as 'a wretched hive of scum and villainy'. For Luke this planet where nothing ever happens is his home; for Han it is a temporary port, a place to escape from when one of his enemies, Jabba the Hut, catches up with him. The leading men's reasons for being on the planet Tatooine and their reactions to it act as a method of characterisation through which we can quickly understand them.

Again on the planet set we see the combination of the familiar and the strange that makes *Star Wars* so effective. Narrative structure and genre characterisation are all satisfyingly familiar but the *mise en scène* is stunning in its unique other-worldliness. For example, Luke, the quintessential American farm boy longing for some excitement in a landscape as flat, rolling and unadventurous as the American prairies, gazes off into the sunset – but this is a world with two suns.

Costume, make-up and props

A huge part of the impact of *Star Wars* comes from the spectacle created by the non-human characters – both the living alien creatures and the 'droids'. In fact, most of the aliens that we see function entirely as spectacle and play no role in the narrative. They are none the less important in establishing the genre and creating the thrill of strangeness/fear of the unknown. These effects are achieved entirely through costume and make-up.

The other function of costume and make-up is to indicate

character. As the narrative of *Star Wars* focuses on action rather than depth of character the characters tend to fall into types, the broadest category being goodies and baddies, and the audience needs to be able to read and categorise the characters quickly and easily. A primary means through which the film-makers achieve this readability is to employ colour symbolism. Darth Vader's pure black costume is symbolic of the forces of evil: Luke and Leia in white symbolise the opposite force for good. There are variations to the rule, however. The soldiers of the Empire, the Storm Troopers, are dressed in clinical white, symbolically the colour of goodness but here this is undermined by the dehumanising effect of the costume that masks and makes uniform any individual features, creating a robotic and menacing effect. Like the workers in Fritz Lang's *Metropolis* (see Chapter 1) they are identical and relentless, and each one that is shot down is replaced by another from a seemingly never-ending supply. The very name 'Storm Trooper', which originates from the Nazi SS, further enhances the sense of an unstoppable army of evil. This link with fascism is paralleled by the grey uniforms of the commanding officers of the *Death Star*, which are strongly reminiscent of the uniforms of both Hitler's and Mussolini's armies in World War II.

The character of Darth Vader has the same clean, clinical lines, deployed in his face mask, as the Storm Troopers. With its sharp, gleaming contours the face mask is both non-human and deeply menacing because of what is hidden from us rather than what we can see.

Vader's opponent, Obi-Wan Kenobi, presents us with a complete contrast in his costume. Instead of the futuristic flowing black robes of Darth Vader he is dressed in a rough-textured monk's habit complete with cowl. Vader's costume suggests a technological future that eliminates the human qualities from the individual; Ben's suggests an ancient past hinting at many religions including the ancient magic of druids, monks, hermits, Buddhist monks and, perhaps most powerfully, the Japanese warrior knights, the samurai. The beam of light cast by his sabre is symbolically a searing blue/white in contrast to Vader's that is red (possibly denoting the Devil).

Leia is almost the only female character, certainly the only one of significance, in the film. There are two distinctive features to her costume, each with specific connotations. The first is the flowing, white robes that she wears. Pure white, the symbol of goodness, the fabric looks both shiny and slippery – a futuristic look, and yet there is the suggestion in the style of its graceful folds of a princess from the *Arabian Nights*. Her costume is austere, modestly covering all flesh like a nun's habit, but the hint of the *Arabian Nights* provides a dash of magic and daring, to her character. The second distinctive feature of Leia's appearance is her hairstyle, which implies a medieval setting (along with the knight/samurai costumes, round table, etc.), at odds with the modern technology and combining to underline the unique otherness of the world of the film. It is one of the features of costume and make-up that locate this film 'a long time ago in a galaxy far, far away'. In *The Phantom Menace* (Lucas USA, 1999) this hairstyle is developed in more Japanese geisha-like directions, suggesting a race and caste apart. The final feature of Leia's costume and make-up that is worthy of comment is the classic Hollywood glamour whereby, in spite of detention, battle and torture, her hair remains perfect, her lip-gloss undimmed – as we would expect of any good heroine in the movies.

Luke, like Leia, is dressed in white. The simple robes denote his youth and innocence. There is also in the style of his costume, as we saw with Ben Kenobi, an echo of the Japanese samurai, indicating the religious/warrior role marked out for him.

Han Solo in contrast, is like a character from a Western. In black and tan complete with gun-belt and holster, he appears more sophisticated and worldly than Luke, his choice of weapon denoting that his sphere of action is the shoot-out rather than the single combat with a magical sabre that is Luke's domain.

These careful and deliberate choices in costume, make-up and props are crucial to the success of the film. They establish the generic context(s), create the sense of other-worldliness that locates the film in space, and define the characters, providing clues to the viewer as to how we should interpret them.

Lighting

Considering that this is a sci-fi fantasy, the use of light in *Star Wars* is relatively naturalistic. The spaceship interiors are lit apparently from the myriad of light sources within. The ships glide through space given an air of verisimilitude by the illumination of the 'stars'. The stars themselves are the beacons of light we all see in the sky at night.

Lucas and cinematographer Gilbert Taylor do allow themselves some expressionist moments, e.g. early on in the film the glow of a sunset illuminates Luke's face at the homestead. There is no doubt that Lucas is both paying tribute to – and subsuming the narrative and philosophical weight of – John Ford's 'Monument Valley' Westerns, especially *The Searchers* (1956).

FIGURE EXPRESSION AND MOVEMENT WITHIN THE FRAME

A particular kind of performance is required in a vehicle like *Star Wars*. The film is not concerned with exploring and portraying subtle nuances of character. Instead the narrative is contrived of a series of 'cliff hangers' where we see the characters engaged in one crisis after another. As these crises involve conflict, pursuit and escape the primary means of expression is through body language. We see the characters engaged in very physical activities. As in the tradition of Westerns (particularly those directed by Howard Hawks) and Akira Kurosawa's 'samurai' films the characters are what they do. Victory belongs to those with the greatest skill with their weapons. The moral message of the film is that such strength and skill belongs to the honourable and the good. Victory is inevitably theirs despite the seemingly invincible might of the Empire. Thus we see performances where choreographed fight scenes provide the most significant moments. Both Ben Kenobi and Luke exhibit the graceful balletic movements of the samurai (see parallels with duels in *Seven Samurai* (Kurosawa, 1954, Japan) and *Yojimbo* (Kurosawa, 1961, Japan) in particular) when fighting with their light sabres.

In the final escape from the *Death Star* Luke takes on the mantle of the Hollywood sword wielders from Douglas Fairbanks to Errol Flynn. His performance becomes ever more swashbuckling as he rescues Leia. Of all the characters Darth Vader is perhaps the one who has to rely on body language to the greatest extent as his face mask excludes the possibility of facial expression. Costume plays a considerable part in establishing his character – including his monumental nature – but the way in which he stands, moves and fights is also crucial. If we look back to his first appearance in the film we can see an example of how the film-makers use careful positioning within the frame to provide his character with an aura of power and menace. We see a long shot of a sealed door on the princess's ship in the centre of the frame. Suspense is created as the shot lingers on the door that is slowly being cut open. Once open we see Vader's figure doubly framed in the doorway and in the centre of the screen. He strides forwards until his figure dominates the frame in full-shot and then pauses for effect. This conventional but effective use of positioning within the frame helps to construct his character and role within the film.

CINEMATOGRAPHY

The positioning of the camera and the use of camera angles in *Star Wars* is consistent with mainstream Hollywood movies since the 1930s. Long shots are used to establish where the action is taking place, to show off the sets and to film battles or large action sequences. Mid-shots and close-ups are used to show reactions and feelings and to define who are the most important characters – thus we see close-ups on the faces of the film's heroes. There are some interesting examples of camera placement and angle. On Darth Vader's first appearance (described above) he strides forward to dominate the frame and then we cut to a low-angle close-up where both the angle and position of the camera emphasise his power and importance. He then demonstrates his strength and ruthlessness by picking a character up by the neck. The camera angle is level but the camera is placed on the floor to show only the legs of the characters. This allows us to focus on the man's boots as they dangle in mid-air. The choice of camera placement thus emphasises Vader's action and his strength.

Throughout the film Lucas and Taylor deliberately distance the camera from the action. Close-ups are less often used than mid-shots. Many scenes are played out almost entirely in full-shot or wider. Mobile camera shots are used sparingly to shadow action. Most of the time the camera keeps its distance and poise. This allows the audience to experience the narrative as a spectacle. This strategy is also of a piece with the film's knowing utilisation of film history, i.e. utilising a shot selection reminiscent of both Ford and Kurosawa.

The crisp, deep-focus quality of image in *Star Wars* is achieved by careful choice of camera and lens. The live action sequences of *Star Wars* were shot by vintage 1950s VistaVision cameras – John

Ford's favourite tool. (After the film was released, these cameras became highly sought after by cinematographers.)

Perhaps the most notable aspect of the film's cinematography, certainly the most famous, is its pioneering use of stop-motion control in filming the battle scenes. The creation of the illusion of vast scale is achieved by using small models and slow motion to make distances and explosions (the two main visual signatures of the film) look vast.

Many shots in *Star Wars* are actually composites of more than one image. The expertise of Lucas's team (which included several people specifically employed on optical matching) brought a new level to picture quality and cohesion. The effect is the highly realistic looking spaceship scenes described at the beginning of this chapter which contribute so much to the spectacle of the film.

Much of the visual effectiveness of the film is a result of work carried out after the filming. The post-production of the movie involved not only the imposition of a myriad of light effects – including the 'sabres' – but a major sound effects and re-recording effort. The credits list for sound on the film is far longer than any other activity. Even the exposed film itself was subject to careful grading and regrading in the developing and printing phase. What would once have been described as 'mistakes' in developing the print helped to further enhance the bleached out exteriors and luminous white interiors captured in the filming.

EDITING

The editing of *Star Wars* – by Richard Chew, Paul Hirsch and Marcia Lucas and supervised by George Lucas himself – follows the grand tradition of Hollywood. Within scenes the editing follows the principles of the continuity system, becoming as unobtrusive as possible. Following the rules of continuity editing, each scene is made up of a combination of different types of shot with the camera moving closer to the action to delineate character, further from the action to establish spatial continuity. Spatial continuity is created and maintained by the use of long shots to establish the space before cutting closer to the action, by adherence to the 30-degree and the 180-degree rules, and the use of shot/reverse shot to film conversations. The pace of editing changes according to the type of action being filmed, tending to become faster in battle/conflict scenes, thereby creating a sense of energy and urgency.

The editing of shots is – as is the case with much post-war American cinema – less closely matched than in the classical Hollywood period. Often sequences are matched/contrasted by material and narrative content rather than purely visual components. Radical changes can be performed by bridges and continuous narrative thread. The most striking feature of the editing of *Star Wars* is the extensive use of the wipe to signify changes of location and/or time frame. Wipes are a very visible method of joining shots. They draw attention to the editing process thus creating a very decisive break between scenes signalling that the action has moved to a new plane.

Enormous attention to the detail in cinematography, post-production and editing are all well and good but as Lucas has put it himself: 'A special effect is a tool, a means of telling a story. A special effect without a story is a pretty boring thing.'

NARRATIVE STRUCTURE

The sub-title of the reissue of *Star Wars* is *Episode IV – A New Hope*. After the issue of the sequel *The Empire Strikes Back* it became clear that that there was to be a series of movies. The original film became part of a sequence of episodes. The structure of the original film's narrative (written by George Lucas) is itself episodic. The opening sequence illustrates this by plunging us straight into the action of a story/adventure coming to its close: the flight, pursuit and capture of Princess Leia. In order to make events comprehensible to the viewer the film starts with written text explaining 'the story so far. . .' Thus in contrast to the beginning/middle/end structure of the classic Hollywood narrative we are clearly starting in the middle of a serialised story.

There are other differences between *Star Wars* and the classic Hollywood narrative. In a classic narrative we would expect the story to be character-driven, with a focus on psychological realism and clear motivation. Whilst the motivation of the characters in the film is clear (if simple) it is debatable whether or not it is the driving force in the film. Many, including Thomas Elsaesser (in Neale and Smith's *Contemporary Hollywood Cinema* (1998)) claim that the film pays less attention to character motivation in order to focus on the visceral, fast-paced action sequences and spectacular effects.

The characters are certainly motivated by very basic goals: Princess Leia wants to save the Universe; Grand Moff Tarkin wants to control it; Darth Vader wants to exercise a dark mystical power. Han is motivated by profit rather than altruism although this changes (without explanation) at the end of the film when he returns in the Falcon to help Luke. The only exception to this simplistic pattern of motivation is Luke whose motives are more clearly defined. Like a Western hero he is motivated by the desire to get revenge for the deaths of his father (as he believes), his aunt and uncle and Ben Kenobi. Once established, however, this motive seems rather to evaporate and the more morally acceptable desire to save the Universe takes over. Perhaps the real (certainly the most evident) motivation of the characters, is the desire to get out of whatever current scrape they are in and on to the next adventure. In this respect the film owes more to the B-movie serials of the 1930s than to classic Hollywood as the narrative moves swiftly from one cliff-hanger to the next.

NARRATIVE PATTERNS

The story of *Star Wars* presents us with a reworking of familiar themes. It is because of this that the film can get away with such slight character motivation. The characters fall into types already familiar to us from a range of fairytales, films, myths and legends. We don't need elaborate motivation; we know who they are already.

Luke's character for example, with his secret parentage and hidden destiny, has many predecessors, not least in Arthurian legend, where the baby Arthur is hidden by Merlin. His true royal identity is only revealed once he pulls the sword from the stone. Further parallels with Arthurian legend are suggested by the use of the title and role of the Jedi Knights who, like the Knights of the Round Table, acted as protectors of the kingdom, physical and moral. Similarly, Obi-Wan Kenobi, with his magic lore and hooded cowl, is reminiscent of Merlin (Arthur's magician). This is but one example. Many other parallels can be found between *Star Wars* and earlier stories, ranging from Greek myth and legend, Victorian melodrama of mistaken identity and betrayal, frontier adventures, television and most obviously to a host of war movies and Westerns.

STAR WARS AND THE MOVIE INDUSTRY

Such a populist, generic and glitzy project as *Star Wars* would surely have appealed to any of the movie moguls of the Hollywood Golden Age. Surely Selznick would have relished a 'no holds barred' epic of an Empire 'Gone with the Jedi'. The production of Star Wars is not a classic Hollywood story because *Star Wars* was not the product of classical Hollywood. It is a post-1948, post-Paramount Hollywood production. As such, 'block-buster' as it became, *Star Wars* was an 'independent' production. Lucas formed a company to produce the film. The costs of such a production would be considerable. In 1975–76 the studios were going through a regular bout of financial conservatism. Lucas could not attract funding for this movie. Much as John Ford could not convince David O. Selznick in 1939 that Westerns had a future, Lucas was faced with an industry that saw sci-fi as box-office poison.

Versions of *Star Wars* were turned down by several studios until Twentieth Century Fox gave Lucas a chance. The studio was in what appeared to be terminal decline. Senior executives were desperate for some success to place on their CVs before they left. Lucas had received attention after his 1973 film *American Graffiti* had won a Golden Globe and five Oscar nominations. He could bring some much needed youthful enthusiasm and the gloss of success to the old studio. The accountants were particularly attracted to the project when Lucas agreed to forgo his directing salary in exchange for 40 per cent of the film's box-office net and all merchandising rights. Merchandising before *Star Wars* was seen as, at best, a nice bonus.

Star Wars was budgeted at a hefty but not spectacular $11 million. In 1975 Kubrick's *Barry Lyndon* had cost a similar amount. Spielberg's *Jaws* had cost 12m. As the production returned from North Africa and went into post-production the executives at Twentieth Century Fox became convinced that *Star Wars* was going to be a disaster. Large amounts of money had already been spent so exit strategies were essayed. They attempted to sell off their stake in the film to anybody willing to listen. There were no takers. At one point some at Fox were keen that the planned (expensive) effects could be removed from the production budget. The whole project could have been a low-budget TV show (following the hugely successful *Star Trek*).

The 'New Hollywood' is less about the mogul's whim and more about – often haphazard and desperate – attempts to pre-guess audience reaction. As the film industry became more and more entwined with the advertising and marketing industry so the focus group (or preview audience) became pre-eminent. Positive feedback from an advanced screening of *Star Wars* made the 'suits' change their minds. The profits from the film ended up saving the studio from bankruptcy.

In its opening weekend *Star Wars* took a solid $1.554 million from a modest 43 screens. The expansion of impact – and income – since has been phenomenal. The real phenomenon of *Star Wars* has been the decision to develop the movie into a series: *The Empire Strikes Back* (1980) was followed by *Return of the Jedi* (1983). After a break – fuelled by speculation and a 'digital' re-release of *Star Wars* itself to remind the initial audience and bring in a new generation – Lucas launched *Star Wars: Episode I – The Phantom Menace* in 1999. *Episode II* (2002) and *Episode III* (2005) will follow. In its opening weekend (February 1997) the reissue of *Star Wars* played on over 2000 screens in the USA and took almost $36 million (USA).

Sequelisation was not a new game in Hollywood – although typically no franchise had ever developed such an all-encompassing mythology around it as Lucas' project. Marketing had always been a major concern for the Hollywood studios. It was, after all, what made them major players at home and abroad. Again Lucas took it further and faster and utilised merchandising in a consistent and all-encompassing way never seen before. Ahead of the field in 1977, Lucas and Co. have continued to lead the way, e.g. in the exploitation of a huge fan-base by utilisation of the World Wide Web (see, for example, *The Star Wars* site: http://www.star-wars.com/episode-iv/).

GENRE

Away from hi-tech marketing and virtual space *Star Wars* has an interesting relationship to the good old-fashioned concept of genre. Many of the characteristics which define genre clearly mark *Star Wars* as a science fiction film. It is mostly in the *mise en scène* that we see this, particularly in the space locations, costume, make-up and props and the use of lighting effects, especially in the creation of battle scenes. In other respects the genre is not so clear. The film's central narrative drive, the conflict between good and evil, though set in space is not unique to the sci-fi genre, neither do we find stars or music that characterise the film as science fiction. In fact *Star Wars* is a prime example of bricolage, i.e. the bringing together of elements of different genres, improvising and adapting to create something new. It is part of the derivative nature of the film that it draws on elements from (World War II) films and Westerns – especially in (adapted) *mise en scène* and narrative characteristics – as well as science fiction. There are specific allusions to a number of films. The bombing raids and dog fights have their origins in films like *The Dam Busters* (Anderson, UK, 1955) and *633 Squadron* (Grauman, UK, 1964). The scene in which Luke returns to his aunt and uncle's burnt-out homestead is more than reminiscent of a similar scene in *The Searchers*. The victory celebration at the end of the film is based on the finale of Leni Riefenstahl's *Triumph of the Will* (1936). Many analysts have noticed a very close resemblance between the whole film and Akira Kurosawa's *Hidden Fortress* (*Kakushi toride no san akunin*, 1958).

Stardom

Unlike much Hollywood product, *Star Wars* was not a star vehicle. The only headline actor to appear in it was Alec Guinness, playing Obi-Wan Kenobi (not really a starring role). All the other performers were relatively unknown at the time the film was made. In spite of the film's enormous success only one, Harrison Ford, went on to become a star, and whilst *Star Wars* has undoubtedly contributed to his star image it was a subsequent film, *Raiders of the Lost Ark* (Spielberg, USA, 1981) that turned him into a star. Perhaps this lack of stars is a reflection of the rather flimsy characterisation and the fact that we have many characters and many episodes competing for our attention rather than a central hero with a starring role. The film was certainly marketed on the strength of its special effects and fantasy *mise en scène* rather than any star image.

AUTEUR

Approaching *Star Wars* as a vehicle for auteur analysis depends on George Lucas' claim to auteur status. That status cannot be achieved through one film. Fortunately Lucas has directed other films (apart from the components of the *Star Wars* franchise), including a good deal of made for television product as well as *THX 1138* (1970) and *American Graffiti* (1973). He has written the material for many films, including the stories for the *Indiana Jones* Trilogy and the spin-off TV series. He is producer of – amongst others – all of the *Star Wars* films.

George Lucas planned to become a professional racing driver. However, a terrible car accident changed his views on life. Whilst convalescing he developed the (admittedly half-baked) idea of 'the force'. He decided to enrol in the University of Southern California film school. As a film student he made several short films including *THX-1138: 4EB (Electronic Labyrinth)* that won first prize at the 1967–68 National Student Film Festival. In 1967 he was awarded a scholarship by Warner Brothers to observe Francis Ford Coppola making *Finian's Rainbow*. Lucas and Coppola became good friends and formed a company called American Zoetrope.

The company's first project was Lucas' full-length version of *THX:1138*. This film – when viewed with the hindsight of *Star Wars* – set the paradigm for Lucas' visual signature and thematic interests. 'THX' (Robert Duvall) attempts to escape from a subterranean futuristic fascist state. In this clinical future (high-key lit, bright white *mise en scène*, photographed with a still distance) love and sex are outlawed. The film encapsulates Lucas' strengths, i.e. clarity and visual élan, with his weaknesses, i.e ponderousness and a lack of believable character development.

In 1971, Coppola went into production of *The Godfather*, thereby developing his own claim to auteur status. Lucas formed his own company, Lucasfilm Ltd. In 1973 he wrote and directed the semi-autobiographical – and critically acclaimed – *American Graffiti*. He began writing the screenplay for *Star Wars*. In 1975 he went so far to establish ILM (Industrial Light & Magic) to produce the visual effects needed for the movie. Another Lucas company called Sprocket Systems (later Skywalker Sound) was established to edit and mix *Star Wars*. Since the release of the first *Star Wars* movie Lucas has carefully developed an ever-extending matrix of actual films, mythology and marketing around 'the force'.

The authorial signature displayed by Lucas ever since has been one of complete control over his product, including the flood of more or less related products that have been sold on the back of the franchise: 'I took over control of the merchandising not because I thought it was going to make me rich, but because I wanted to control it. I wanted to make a stand for social, safety, and quality reasons. I didn't want someone using the name "Star Wars" on a piece of junk.'

On a more prosaic level we could claim that the Lucas signature since his first movie is the ubiquitous use of the letters/numbers 'THX 1138', e.g. the licence plate number on Milner's deuce coupé in *American Graffiti* (1973), Lucas' own sound system – now dominating top-flight cinemas across the globe – is named THX, a battle android who captures Jar Jar Binks in *The Phantom Menace* has the number 1138 written on his back. Thus in *Star Wars*, Luke Skywalker refers to Chewbacca as 'Prisoner transfer from cell block 1138'.

REPRESENTATION

Although ostensibly set 'a long time ago in a galaxy far, far away' *Star Wars* is of course an American film with American actors taking the lead roles. In many respects it follows the characteristics of the Western genre (a genre which traditionally presents us with America's reflections upon itself), the difference being that the frontier has moved from the Wild West to space. Given the world-wide impact of the film it is particularly important to look at the underlying messages it presents about gender, race, class and nation. We can do this by looking at the qualities and values the film is endorsing (through association with the heroes). We then need to consider whether national, racial, gender or class characteristics are being connected with these values.

Representation of nation

We can start with the triad of characters at the heart of the film: Luke, Han and Leia. These three characters embody the qualities of bravery, skill, courage, altruism and humour. In other words they are good. They are also in accent and appearance white and American – a fact that might lead to the belief that white

Americans embody these positive qualities, or that only white Americans embody these qualities. This of course depends on theories of how the audience consumes the text (see Chapter 10). Let us compare this with the villains of the film. Darth Vader, Grand Moff Tarkin, in fact all the agents of the Empire appear European in accent and/or appearance. As villains they represent greed, ruthlessness and tyranny – values that are clearly being divorced from any American characteristics. This kind of representation has earned criticism for Lucas (most recently with *The Phantom Menace*, in which the bumbling, cowardly Ja Ja Binks has a Caribbean accent).

Representation of gender

So far Princess Leia has been included with her two male counterparts and she certainly exhibits some of the same qualities that they do. She is both courageous and altruistic. She doesn't give in to torture. Unlike the female characters in most Westerns, she seizes a weapon and joins in with the fighting. So far we might think that the film represents women as equal to men, allowing them a more extensive sphere of action than has been traditional (i.e. wife/mother or siren/whore). However, although Leia, not Luke or Han, is ostensibly the leader of this small band of heroes this is because of her Royal status rather than any leadership skills and this status is consistently undermined by Han's satirical comments, e.g. 'your worshipfulness'. We see her being bossy but not particularly competent. Like the archetypal damsel in distress she starts the film by needing to be rescued. Once this rescue is achieved her role becomes that of flirtatious counterpart to Han Solo and cheerleader to Luke when he flies off to defeat the enemy.

It is significant that we have to base an analysis of the representation of women almost entirely upon Leia. Women's absence from this sphere of action (predominantly battle/conflict/adventure) itself suggests that this is not a suitable female domain. There is, however, one other female character who makes a brief appearance: Luke's aunt. She is softly spoken and gentle. We see her cooking food for Luke and his uncle and presiding over the family meal. When Luke's uncle appears harsh she defends Luke in a nurturing, maternal fashion, pleading tolerance and understanding. The setting in which we see her may be strange, even alien to us but the characteristics of the good wife and mother are not.

Looking at the representation of these two women together it would seem that the film is endorsing some roles for women but not others – the good wife/mother figure, the companion and encourager of men. Leia may be a domineering princess, not frightened to express herself, but her primary function within the narrative remains that of the source of motivation for male action, i.e. the damsel in distress.

CONCLUSION

Star Wars has served as our 'text' for the various concepts and constructs of studying film that we have introduced in this book. The various aspects of film and the various ways of studying them are presented as tools for use. Film is a multifarious and multi-layered medium, open to a vast range of viewing. The point of film studies – and indeed of this volume – is to advance and utilise various approaches to enhance our understanding/appreciation of this or of any film. It is our fondest hope that readers will enter 'the kingdom of the shadows' – whether to find a 'galaxy far, far away' or that 'there's no place like home' – to appreciate, understand AND ENJOY more.

Recommended reading and viewing

The following films and books are recommended as illustrative and source material for the study of the areas and concepts we have covered in this book. The lists are not prescriptive and are far from exhaustive. They are simply a starting point, using materials that are easily available, i.e. films that are available commercially on video and books that are in print.

Chapter 1 – Mise en scène

Viewing

To see *mise en scène* used as a storytelling medium:
   Metropolis (Lang, Germany, 1926)
   Raiders of the Lost Ark (Spielberg, USA, 1981)
The use of colour is highlighted in:
   The Wizard of Oz (Fleming, USA, 1939)
   Wings of Desire (Wenders, Germany, 1987)
 Light as a tool for film-makers can be seen to particular effect in:
   Days of Heaven (Malik, USA, 1978)

Chapter 2 – Cinematography

Viewing

   Citizen Kane (Welles, USA, 1940)
   The Third Man (Reed, UK, 1949)
   The Seven Samurai (Kurosawa, Japan, 1954)
   Touch of Evil (Welles, USA, 1958)
   Raging Bull (Scorsese, USA, 1980)
The American Film Institute has produced the video *Visions of Light* (1993) in which world famous cinematographers talk about their art.

Chapter 3 – Editing

Viewing

Battleship Potemkin (Eisenstein, USSR, 1926)
The Man With the Movie Camera (Vertov, USSR, 1929)
To Have and Have Not (Hawks, USA, 1940)
Breathless (Godard, France, 1959)
Psycho (Hitchcock, USA, 1960)

Chapter 4 – Narrative

Viewing

Early cinema's growth into narrative complexity is well covered
by the BFI video collection *Primitives and Pioneers* (1990).

Casablanca (Curtiz, USA, 1940)
Rashomon (Kurosawa, Japan, 1950)
Bad Timing (Roeg, UK, 1979)
Pulp Fiction (Tarantino, USA, 1994)
Run Lola Run (Tykwer, Germany, 1998)

Reading

D. Bordwell *Narration in the Fiction Film* (London, 1985)
D. Bordwell and K. Thompson *Film Art: An Introduction* (latest
edition)

Chapter 5 – Classical Hollywood

Viewing

'Hollywood' in its classical era was a factory so there are many
thousands of films to choose from.

'The' Hollywood Movie is *Casablanca* (Curtiz, USA, 1942)
The classical reaches its baroque form with *Gone With the Wind*
(Fleming, USA, 1939)
Martin Scorsese's *Personal Journey through American Movies*
(1996) is a 'must see' for any student of the subject.

Reading

D. Bordwell and K. Thompson *Film History* (New York, 1994)

D. Bordwell, J. Staiger and K. Thompson *The Classical Hollywood Cinema: Film Style and Mode of Production to 1960* (London, 1985)
S. Neale and M. Smith (eds) *Contemporary Hollywood* (London, 1998)
A. Higson and R. Maltby *Film Europe and Film America* (Exeter, 1999)
G. Nowell Smith and S Ricci (eds) *Hollywood and Europe* (London, 1998)

Chapter 6 – Outside Hollywood

Viewing

Battleship Potemkin and *Ivan the Terrible* (Eisenstein, USSR, 1925 and 1942–46)
The Man With the Movie Camera (Vertov, USSR, 1929)
Rome – Open City (Rossellini, Italy, 1945)
The Bicycle Thieves (De Sica, Italy, 1949)
The 400 Blows (available on video with *The Brats*) (Truffaut, France, 1959) *Breathless* (Godard, France, 1959)
Paris vu Par (Godard *et al.*, France, 1963) – an interesting collection of shorts by several of the *Nouvelle Vague* auteurs.
The Idiots (von Trier, Denmark, 1998)
Celebration (Vinterberg, Denmark, 1998)

Reading

R. Taylor and I. Christie (eds) *The Film Factory* (London, 1994)
R. Taylor and I. Christie (eds) *Inside the Film Factory* (London, 1994)
S. Hayward *French National Cinema* (London, 1993)
P. Sorlin *Italian National Cinema* (London, 1997)
R. Kelly *The Name of this Book Is Dogma 95* (London, 2000)
The BFI Encyclopaedia of European Cinema (London, 1997)
Alternatives to Hollywood can of course be seen operating in a number of national and regional cinemas, e.g. South-East Asia and particularly Hong Kong and Taiwan. For an introduction to the latter we recommend:
D. Bordwell *Planet Hollywood* (London, 2000)
An excellent general introduction is available in:
J. Hill and P. Gibson (eds) *World Cinema: Critical Studies* (Oxford, 2000)

Chapter 7 – Genre

Viewing

We have chosen to look at the Western. It is in the nature of genre analysis that any *type* of film will do. Remember, genre study requires study of a number of films over an extended period of time. Thus, for the Western we recommend:

The Great Train Robbery (Porter, USA, 1903)
Stagecoach (Ford, USA, 1939)
The Searchers (Ford, USA, 1956)
High Noon (Zinnemann, USA, 1952)
Rio Bravo (Hawks, USA, 1959)
McCabe and Mrs Miller (Altman, USA, 1971)
The Wild Bunch (Pekinpah, USA, 1969)
Unforgiven (Eastwood, USA, 1992)

Reading

R. Altman *Film/Genre* (London, 1999)
E. Buscombe (ed.) *The BFI Companion to the Western* (London, 1988)
B. K. Grant *Film Genre Reader I* and *Genre Reader II* (Texas, 1986 and 1995)

Chapter 8 – Stardom

Viewing

The choice of subject for an analysis of stardom – has to be a personal one.

NB: for analysis it is probably best to pick one that is not a favourite (otherwise a certain amount of critical distance may be lost). Remember it is not just the films – *look at the subsidiary forms of communication.*

Reading

C. Gledhill (ed.) *Star Signs* (London, 1992)
R. Dyer *Stars* (London, 1980)
R. Dyer *Heavenly Bodies: Film Stars and Society* (London, 1986)
D. Thomson *The Biographical Dictionary of Film* (London, 1995)

provides an informative and opinionated reference book for all biographical enquiry.

Chapter 9 – Auteur

Viewings should be of as wide a range as possible. It is impossible to 'do' an auteur without at least five or six films (preferably from more than one genre) to look at for characteristics.

Reading

In such a quintessentially personal area of film studies once again David Thomson's *Biographical Dictionary of Film* (London, 1995) is a fine starting point.

J. Caughie (ed.) *Theories of Authorship* (London, 1981)

Chapter 10 – Medium and Message

Texts used for analysis of representation should rely on the personal choice and experience of the analyst. Some books that might help you are:

J. Ellis *Visible Fictions* (London, 1982)

D. Gauntlett *Moving Experiences* (London, 1995)

E. A. Kaplan (ed.) *Psychoanalysis and Film* (London, 1990)

A. Kuhn *The Power of the Image* (London, New York, 1985)

R. Lapsley and M. Westlake *Film Theory* (Manchester, 1992)

J. Lechte *Fifty Key Contemporary Thinkers* (London, 1994)

J. Stacey *Star Gazing. Hollywood Cinema and Female Spectatorship* (London, 1993)

FURTHER READING

The field of film studies is not one undersupplied with study guides and textbooks. This is a selection of the best of them.

D. Bordwell and K. Thompson's *Film Art* and *Film History* (latest editions)

S. Hayward *Cinema Studies: The Key Concepts* (London, 2000)

J. Hill and P. Church Gibson *Oxford Guide to Film Studies* (Oxford, 1998)
J. Monaco *How to Read a Film* (London, 2000)

Index of films, personalities and movements